Leading with Intent

Leading with Intent

Lessons from the Field in School Leadership

Andrew R. Dolloff, PhD

BLOOMSBURY ACADEMIC
NEW YORK • LONDON • OXFORD • NEW DELHI • SYDNEY

BLOOMSBURY ACADEMIC
Bloomsbury Publishing Inc, 1359 Broadway, New York, NY 10018, USA
Bloomsbury Publishing Plc, 50 Bedford Square, London, WC1B 3DP, UK
Bloomsbury Publishing Ireland, 29 Earlsfort Terrace, Dublin 2, D02 AY28, Ireland

BLOOMSBURY, BLOOMSBURY ACADEMIC and the Diana logo are
trademarks of Bloomsbury Publishing Plc

First published in the United States of America 2026

Copyright © Andrew R. Dolloff, 2026

AASA Logo © The School Superintendents Association (AASA)
Cover images: © iStock/ EtiAmmos

All rights reserved. No part of this publication may be: i) reproduced or transmitted in any form, electronic or mechanical, including photocopying, recording or by means of any information storage or retrieval system without prior permission in writing from the publishers; or ii) used or reproduced in any way for the training, development or operation of artificial intelligence (AI) technologies, including generative AI technologies. The rights holders expressly reserve this publication from the text and data mining exception as per Article 4(3) of the Digital Single Market Directive (EU) 2019/790.

Bloomsbury Publishing Inc does not have any control over, or responsibility for, any third-party websites referred to or in this book. All internet addresses given in this book were correct at the time of going to press. The author and publisher regret any inconvenience caused if addresses have changed or sites have ceased to exist, but can accept no responsibility for any such changes.

A catalog record for this book is available from the Library of Congress

ISBN: HB: 978-1-4758-7525-6
       PB: 978-1-4758-7526-3
       ePDF: 979-8-8818-6809-3
       eBook: 978-1-4758-7527-0

Typeset Integra Software Services Pvt. Ltd.
Printed and bound in the United States of America

For product safety related questions contact productsafety@bloomsbury.com.

To find out more about our authors and books visit www.bloomsbury.com
and sign up for our newsletters.

For Mom—who was a much stronger force than we ever realized.

And for Scott Aaron White—my childhood confidante, bumper pool nemesis, and wiffleball teammate extraordinaire, who became an outstanding school leader in his own right.

Contents

List of Figures viii
List of Tables ix
Acknowledgments xi
Preface xii

1 The Call for Trust 1
2 Culture Trumps Structure 9
3 Approaches to Leadership 21
4 Mission-Driven Trust 37
5 Authentic Visibility 57
6 Planning for Transition or Renewal 69
7 Fostering Trust Through Professional Development 87
8 Negotiating with Trust 103
9 Building Student Trust 119
10 Family Connections 135
11 Community Engagement 145
12 Strategic Planning: Preparing to Plan 155
13 Strategic Planning: Creating the Plan 171
14 Strategic Planning: Putting the Plan to Work 193
15 Leading with Intent 205

Bibliography 213
About the Author 215

Figures

14.1 Strategic Plan Implementation 201
A.1 Andrew Dolloff, PhD 215

Tables

3.1	Leadership Theories	22
4.1	Mission Inventory	54
6.1	Phase One: Listening & Learning	75
6.2	Phase Two: Listening, Learning, & Leading	79
7.1	Teacher Professional Development Survey	90
7.2	Unconference Agenda	95
8.1	Negotiations Timeline	111
8.2	Negotiations Protocols	112
8.3	Meeting Norms	113
12.1	Sample School Board Charge to the Strategic Planning Team	162
12.2	Timeline and Planning Process	165
12.3	Potential Data Points	167
13.1	Sample Agenda: Planning Team Meeting I	173
13.2	Sample Agenda: Planning Team Meeting II	174
13.3	Sample Agenda: Public Forum 3—Part A	178
13.4	Sample Agenda: Public Forum 3—Part B	178
13.5	Tips for a Successful Public Forum	180
13.6	Sample Strategic Planning Survey	182

13.7 Sample Agenda: Planning Team Meeting III 185
14.1 Operations Matrix 197
15.1 School Leader Self-Assessment 207
15.2 School Leader Constituent Feedback 209

Acknowledgments

I am indebted to so many who helped to make this book a reality, including hundreds of school leaders with whom I worked over the past four decades. From my own father (who was my high school principal) to those I worked for and, finally, to those I worked alongside; each of them had an impact on the development of my leadership style and philosophy, and I thank them all for their dedication to this work.

Thanks must go to each of the leaders who were coaxed into sharing some of their stories in this book. I won't name each of them here, as they are clearly identified in the chapters that follow. None of them submitted their work expecting to be lauded as a perfect leader; it is risky to share your thoughts in even the most intimate of settings, let alone in work that will be published for others to critique. I am incredibly grateful for their willingness to "put themselves out there" to offer you a glimpse into their expertise.

To Carrie Brandon and her team at Bloomsbury, I offer my deepest thanks. Their assistance in bringing this book from my random thoughts to a finished product has once again been impressively efficient and incredibly helpful.

Of course, the inspiration for all my work continues to come from our ever-growing family. Mariah—an amazing daughter whose professionalism and grit are matched only by her passion for having fun and her empathy for others. Caleb—my free-spirited SoCal surfer son whose love of life and desire to help others are evident to everyone he meets. And Megan and Kristen—two amazing stepdaughters who have only brought more love and joy into my life with each passing year.

Most importantly, to Brenda—my talented and endlessly patient wife with a discerning eye, whose forty-year teaching career prepared her well to serve as the final editor for each of my books. I know how fortunate I am. You can put your red pen away, now, honey.

Preface

Shortly after publishing *The Trust Imperative* in 2022, I had the opportunity to travel around the United States working with PreK-12 school leaders in a variety of settings.[1] From consulting with a handful of school leaders in one small town in northern Maine to speaking in front of hundreds of superintendents in southern California—with many stops in-between—the experience reaffirmed for me what I had long believed to be true:

- Leadership is leadership—no matter where it occurs or in what setting
- The challenges faced by *each* of us are similar to the challenges faced by *all* of us, even though the topics and the players change from place to place
- The solutions to those challenges are likely not unique nor revolutionary but are typically easily defined and replicable

School leaders throughout the country—and beyond our borders as well—continue to take on problems that require intentional, consistent effort. Even when faced with new challenges, we must realize that we are not alone, and it is likely others have passed this way before us.

Therefore, I set about writing this book as a follow-up to *The Trust Imperative* to highlight some of the work being done by experienced leaders who have been recognized by their peers as leaders among leaders. In these pages, you will find not only suggestions I have made based on my own three decades of experience, constantly borrowing and stealing ideas from my colleagues, but also examples of effective leadership strategies shared directly from our colleagues throughout the United States and internationally.

Nothing about school leadership is rocket science. I say that with the greatest respect for the profession and those who endeavor to make it their career. The work is hard—there is no question about that. But it's not an overly intellectual endeavor; if it were, I would likely not have remained employed for the past thirty years. Knowing what to do and when to do it is the easy part. Having the professional willpower, the courage, and the integrity to implement effective strategies is the more challenging aspect of the work.

This text, then, is aimed at empowering you to explore ideas that you may or may not have considered before, and to recommit yourself to those values and approaches that will allow you to most effectively impact change and further your school's mission. My hope is that you will find here a few nuggets of wisdom that may help you refine your practice or inspire you to rededicate yourself to a trust-based approach to school leadership. If that happens in the simplest of ways for a small number of readers, this project will have been worth the effort.

Andrew Dolloff, PhD
Gorham, Maine
March 2025

Note

1 Dolloff, A., *The Trust Imperative: Practical Approaches to Effective School Leadership* (Baltimore, MD: Rowman & Littlefield, 2022).

1 The Call for Trust

Trust. Easily broken, difficult to foster ... yet absolutely essential in any people-oriented organization. And let's face it; most organizations are people-oriented (and will remain so if we can hold Artificial Intelligence at bay), none more so than our PreK-12 schools. So long as the intellectual, social, and physical development of students remains at the center of what they do, it is difficult to imagine a time when schools will not be people-oriented.

In any school, the level of trust constituents have in the organization will go a long way toward empowering the school to meet its mission and goals. The challenge for you, the educational leader, is to build trust through every interaction you have with others, as constituents will leave each setting either trusting you more or trusting you less than they did before the interaction. That's human nature, and education is a human business. The earlier in your leadership career you can come to understand how trust is fostered—and how it is broken—the sooner you can begin to lead with intent, building trust each step of the way.

Make no mistake about it, fostering trust in leadership and in the school will be no easy task—especially given the starting point from which many constituents begin to interface with schools and their leaders. As you'll read here—and as you've no doubt gleaned from your perusal of news outlets over the past decade or more, trust is not something the general public gives easily, nor is it something employees automatically provide in every setting to their employers, despite their desire to work in an environment that encourages them to do so.

On a national level, data from the Pew Research Center illustrate a consistently declining level of trust in government by US citizens since the mid-1960s—shortly after the Bay of Pigs disaster and the assassination of John F. Kennedy, followed by the Tet Offensive that unveiled the true extent of America's involvement in the Vietnam Conflict. Prior to those events, nearly 80 percent of Americans expressed confidence in the nation's government to "do the right thing." As the 1960s ended, social upheaval and the assassinations of Martin Luther King and Robert F. Kennedy shook the country's confidence in the leaders who were left to fill the void. By the time the Watergate scandal resulted in the resignation of President Nixon in 1974, Americans' trust in public institutions had dropped to 36 percent.[1]

Fast forward fifty years to 2024, and a 36 percent trust rating would be considered superior, as American government has not enjoyed a vote of confidence of that magnitude since 2005. In fact, according to Pew data, nearly 80 percent of Americans now express a healthy distrust of government—and have done so for two decades.

The level of affirmation enjoyed by public officials in the 1950s, when 80 percent of Americans inherently trusted their public leaders, seems unimaginable in today's world of polarization, narcissism, and paranoia. Today, leaders in the public and private sectors are one email, one soundbite, or one social media post away from losing credibility and, possibly, their job, as the demand for perfection and intolerance for viewpoints different from those of the most aggressive critics can lead to viral campaigns that leave the organization with few options other than a change in leadership.

Fortunately, local schools have enjoyed confidence levels nearly double those of the government during recent decades. Research conducted by Phi Delta Kappa International (PDK) reveals that trust has typically been higher for local schools than it has been for the government in general.[2] Respondents have consistently reported confidence in their community schools at a level of approximately 50 percent for forty-eight years, despite a one-year drop to 30 percent in 1984—just after the release of *A Nation at Risk*, the government-directed expose in which "failing" American schools were identified as the greatest threat to the nation's democracy.[3]

Many Americans quickly saw through that early attempt to privatize the country's public schools and responded to the PDK survey based on their own experiences, and trust in schools rebounded to nearly 50 percent the following year. Still, while a 50 percent approval rating might be remarkably high for a government official, it doesn't feel like a strong showing in the world of academia, where a grade of 50 is not close to "meeting the standard." Add to that the PDK data reporting that just 16 percent of US adults have a high level of trust in their community's teachers, and it is clear we have a lot of work to do.

More encouraging is the fact that parents rate their own children's schools higher than the general public does, with approximately 70 percent of parents giving their child's school an A or B rating. While no educator would say that our work is done when we reach a 70 percent success rate, it does provide some reason for optimism and a solid base from which to begin this intentional work of fostering greater trust in our schools.

Researchers and authors have consistently identified trust as the key factor in organizational success. Paul Zak's work at Claremont University explores the connections between brain chemistry and work in high-trust environments. Zak, a neuroscientist, draws the conclusion that employees in trusted workplaces are more consistently present, more fully engaged, more productive, and more satisfied with their lives than workers in low-trust environments.[4]

Imagine a school full of teachers and support personnel who personify Zak's learnings, a place of learning where staff attendance and retention are high, where commitment to the mission is strong, and where classes and staff meetings are filled with optimism and enthusiasm. And then, after dreaming about that for a bit, think about your students and the fact that they, too, are human beings, with brain compositions no different (albeit less fully formed) than that of your staff members. There is every reason to believe that Zak's findings are as applicable to students as they are to adults—if not more so.

We can easily extrapolate Zak's findings to assume that when students attend a school in which they have a high level of trust, they will want to be there—and while there, they will fully engage in lessons from energetic teachers, alongside supportive classmates—all focused on achieving the school's mission while living out its core values.

This sounds like a utopia, for sure. Cynicism might lead us to believe that schools like that simply don't exist—or if they do, they only exist in communities of certain demographics that have reason for optimism. But school leaders must not accept that narrative, lest we underestimate the impact schools have on the lives of our students and on the broader community as a whole.

For some students, the school may be the safest, most affirming place they visit each day. They may come from a place of broken trust, with any number of challenges that make their home or neighborhood an unsafe space. For these students, it is even more critical that school is a safe harbor—a place of trust that provides students not only a space that *is* safe but one in which each student *feels* safe.

How do we get there? How do we create a culture of trust and a school where students and staff want to be present and fully engaged every day? It won't happen by accident; it begins with intentionality. It begins with school leaders who understand that in every interaction they have with others—be it students, staff, or families—they either build trust or degrade trust in themselves and in the organization.

When leaders enter meetings believing they should have the answers, rather than seeking to understand the problem, trust is eroded. When leaders fabricate an answer to something they're not entirely sure of—when they say they'll do something, and it doesn't happen—when they leave student and teacher voices out of decisions that are important to the wider audience—all these things lead to a reduced level of trust in the school.

On the other hand, unfailingly inviting input from others, being consistently inquisitive and empathetic of others, and demonstrating unquestionable integrity are the hallmarks of a leader who understands what it means to foster trust. As we'll explore in later chapters, these leaders create the culture that allows organizational structures to capitalize on that trust, exponentially increasing the school's leadership capabilities, rather than minimizing them to one person or a handful of individuals who lead because of their title.

None of this is new understanding. It's certainly not rocket science. But that doesn't mean it's easy. Often, the challenge in school leadership is not knowing *what* to do, it's having the patience, courage, and humility to see it through. In Jim Collins' classic leadership text, *Good to Great*, he states it a bit differently, reminding us that the most effective leaders are those who demonstrate both personal humility and professional will—facilitating the organization's commitment to its mission while seeking no personal recognition during the effort.[5]

Take, for example, the first-year high school principal faced with the dilemma of a parental complaint about a veteran teacher who refused to accept their student's long-term project because it was submitted fifteen minutes after the deadline that had been communicated at the start of the semester. By the teacher's rule, the tardy submission means that the student will receive no credit for the project, resulting in a failing grade for the course.

The parent argues that the student's excused illness should have negated the need for the paper to be submitted on that date at all, while the teacher argues that she had made it clear that the deadline was the deadline, regardless of the reason for one's absence. Meanwhile, the student's academic record hangs in the balance.

The principal likely knows what to do in this case (hopefully, navigating a compromise in which the teacher recognizes that student learning has occurred, and the harshness of the penalty does not fit the offense), but accomplishing the task won't be easy. It is not likely that the new leader has had a great deal of time to build trust—and the veteran teacher is likely to have a supportive group of colleagues who will argue that any softening of her position is a lowering of standards.

When I use this as a case study with graduate students pursuing a degree in school leadership, participants easily identify the steps they would take to resolve the conflict. In fact, they write their answers with a great deal of conviction, convinced that their approach is best—whether it is to unequivocally support the teacher or the student—or to find some sort of compromise. However, when the setting moves from a case study on a piece of paper to a real-life situation with real personalities, real relationships, and real consequences at stake, one's willingness and ability to commit to doing what is right are often impacted by the attraction of doing what is comfortable.

By creating a trust-filled culture, school leaders face fewer of these difficult dilemmas—and when such conflicts arise there is a clearer path to resolution because the culture provides a consistent definition of what the organization stands for. The challenge is to develop and implement practices that demonstrate intentionality and turn trust-building behaviors into everyday habits.

Fortunately, school leaders need not reinvent the wheel. As I have traveled around the country speaking with school leaders about the call for trust, one thing has become very clear: we are all embroiled in similar daily challenges. Sure, some leaders face certain difficulties on a more frequent or less frequent basis, depending on the nature of the community in which they are working, but the topics from one region of the country to another are relatively consistent.

Because of that consistency, it is likely that a problem vexing one school is concurrently being addressed by many others—providing a community of experts from whom we each can learn. In presentations made to aspiring and veteran school leaders, I often remind them that the most successful strategies we implemented were not the first of their kind but were, in fact, ideas we adapted from others. Notice the use of the word *adapted*, rather than *adopted*, because while you may hear of an idea that works wonderfully in a nearby school, implementation in your own setting will likely require modification to best serve the needs in your community.

Without fail, school leaders can—and should—turn to one another for exemplars and models that improve practice. Too often, we wait for the next conference or hope for a timely book or journal article that addresses an area of need, when all we may need to do is turn to our colleagues—near or far—who have experienced similar challenges. Learning from one another's successes—and failures—is a practical and efficient way to refine performance and develop more impactful leadership practices.

With the focus of nationwide peer coaching in mind, this book is a collection of exemplars from experienced school leaders who have taken the risk to share their ideas with all of us. Each chapter will introduce an area in which school leaders must work to foster trust—with students, staff, families, and communities, to name a few. We will then turn to experts in the field—school leaders from throughout the country—who have graciously and humbly agreed to share one or more practices they have employed to build trust in various settings.

The opportunity to learn from peers should not be as unique as this book proposes; colleagues from down the road or the other side of the globe may be the best resources in this effort, and it is exciting to provide this learning opportunity to newcomers, veterans, and everyone in between.

Special thanks go to the many contributors to this text. None of them offered their experiences claiming to be all-knowing experts. In fact, some of them had to be pestered several times before deciding it would be easier to submit their ideas rather than continue to field requests. In the end, they each appreciated that their experience may help others find greater success in positively impacting the lives of their students.

We'll begin our learning by exploring how school culture sets the tone for learning and is the single most important job of the leader. After a few chapters exploring how to create culture, we will then spend some time looking at exemplary structures that school leaders have implemented to help their schools produce extraordinary results. Finally, three chapters detailing the strategic planning process can be used to set your school on a deliberate path to continual improvement.

While the book is structured to build trust in a manner that is most logical to the author, feel free to skip around and look for chapters and topics that are more pertinent to your current situation. In the end, you should find at least a few ideas that help you take your leadership and your school to new heights.

For Thought and Discussion
1. How well do you believe your school is trusted by your community? What evidence do you have to support that belief? (Have you conducted surveys or asked for specific feedback in this area?)
2. How do events at the national or state level impact the level of trust with which your community views your school? Can you identify specific moments where something that has occurred far away from your schools has had an impact on the culture within the school? How could you respond in a way that fosters trust at that moment?
3. Identify two to three events that have taken place within your own school(s) in the past five years that challenged the level of trust with which others view your leadership or the school. How did the response to those events foster or harm trust in the school? What might you do differently if that event were to occur again?
4. When have you had the occasion to adopt effective programming you have heard about from other schools? How did you alter the programming to fit your school's specific needs? If you were to turn to other schools for examples of programming you might emulate, where would you be most likely to look?

5. Do you think it's fair to say that students will perform better if they are attending a school in which they have a great deal of trust, versus one in which they have little faith? Have you seen this to be true in your own experience? What does it look like when students trust in the school?

Notes

1 "Public Trust in Government: 1958–2024," *Pew Research Center*, last modified (June 24, 2024), https://www.pewresearch.org/politics/2024/06/24/public-trust-in-government-1958-2024/.
2 "Poll of the Public's Attitudes Toward the Public Schools 2022," *Phi Delta Kappa*, last modified (June 25, 2022), https://pdkpoll.org/2022-pdk-poll-results/.
3 Gardner, D. P., *A Nation at Risk: The Imperative for Educational Reform. An Open Letter to the American People. A Report to the Nation and the Secretary of Education*. National Commission on Excellence in Education (ED) (Washington, DC, April 1983). Retrieved from https://eric.ed.gov/?id=ED226006.
4 Zak, P. J., *Trust Factor: The Science of Creating High-Performance Companies* (New York: AMACOM, 2017).
5 Collins, J., *Good to Great: Why Some Companies Make the Leap . . . and Others Don't* (London: Harper Business, 2001).

2 Culture Trumps Structure

"Culture eats strategy for breakfast." These words of wisdom from the 1950s that are often attributed to Peter Drucker, an Austrian American management consultant, educator, and author, still ring true seven decades later. They also apply perfectly to our work in schools, even though Drucker focused his theories on corporate settings.

Drucker didn't offer this theory to imply that strategy and organizational structures are not important. He recognized that strategy and structures are a much-needed part of the trust-building processes organizations employ. Rather, he spoke of the critical importance of the collaborative culture of empowerment that must exist for an organization to travel a more efficient route toward success.

Without a culture of trust, even the most creative and well-defined strategies and structures will fail to allow an organization to operate at its greatest potential. In fact, it's a logical argument that the façade presented by leaders who tout effective strategies without nurturing an authentic culture of trust actually leads to the effective breakdown of the organization. In other words, claiming to implement collaborative strategies, as many leaders do, while paying little attention to the input provided through those structures, does more to degrade trust than simply admitting that your leadership style is not collaborative in the first place.

It is interesting that many think things are different in today's educational setting than they were in Drucker's corporate setting of the 1950s. While it is commonly said that "teachers are different today," the colleagues I worked with in the 1980s were no less interested in collaboration and trust than teachers in our schools today. Just like teachers one-quarter of the way through the twenty-first century, those in the late 1900s desired leaders who acted with integrity, respect, and authenticity while seeking input from employees throughout the school.

With that in mind, there is much to be gleaned from Drucker's simple, catchy phrase. In unpacking his summary statement, leaders find motivation to shift their thinking—and their efforts—toward things that matter. At a minimum, accepting Drucker's philosophy to be true could lead to a re-prioritization of school improvement efforts. Most notably, we are reminded that the best ideas and proposed solutions in any organization will be for naught if leadership has not fostered a mission-focused culture of collegiality and meaningful interpersonal relationships.

To go even further in this analysis, Drucker hit upon the crux of the trust platform that serves as the foundation of this book. Too often, we see schools where strategies exist in abundance, but the lack of integrity in implementing those strategies with authenticity leads to a degradation of trust, as constituents make remarks such as:

- *"Well, they say they value our input, but where's the proof? That committee was just another waste of time."*
- *"I have served on several interview teams, and they never hired the person we wanted, so why bother?"*
- *"That advisory council was just lip service; they didn't really consider any of our ideas. I'm just going to stay in my classroom, close the door, and teach my kids."*

In these brief samples, the *structures* were in place—whether it be interview teams, advisory councils, or other opportunities for input—but the *culture* was lacking; the end result made people feel as though they wasted their time and energy. They felt ignored, dismissed, and patronized. Because they were told they had a voice and then made to feel that their voice was not heard, they had less trust in the organization than they would if they had not been given false hope in the first place. When this happens, human nature is for individuals to begin operating in their own self-interest rather than with the best interest of the school in mind.

Take, for example, a school where Professional Learning Communities (PLCs) are touted as an important part of the weekly schedule. When created, it was stated that PLCs would provide opportunities for teacher collaboration and review of student work in a non-evaluative setting, with the added benefit of offering staff opportunities to experiment with innovative instructional approaches.

Shortly after the PLCs were formed, however, it became clear to staff that leadership was disengaged, taking a laissez-faire approach to the staff's work. While claiming to be operating with a "hands-off" approach, the administration spent little time checking in with PLC leaders, visiting PLC meetings, or collaboratively developing PLC goals and agendas for the year. When PLCs met, administrators stayed in their offices, completing their own tasks, content that the teachers were engaged in their own work.

With no follow-up from leadership, PLC time devolved into complaint sessions—with teachers often doing individual classroom work, correcting papers, entering grades, and planning lessons while PLC leaders attempted to facilitate collaboration. While the *structure* was in place for effective PLC work, the *culture* within the school created a situation in which PLCs became "forced meeting time" that teachers viewed as detracting from their own planning time, rather than adding to the richness of the school's offerings. In effect, implementing the strategy without addressing the culture led to a greater lack of trust throughout the school than would have existed if PLCs had not been formed at all.

Unfortunately, this is commonplace in schools. We often hear school leaders promoting their latest strategy or structure, yet when we speak with constituents in their school, a disconnect is revealed. The reason for this may be the same as why many schools focus their school improvement efforts on revising curriculum rather than improving instruction and school culture; sitting in an office, creating plans, and developing structures on paper are a lot easier than building relationships and improving culture, which require face-to-face interactions and effort.

We see this over and over again in the curriculum review process. In a common example, a school leader reviews student performance and sees a decline in math scores in the third grade. The immediate reaction is to revamp the curriculum, select a new textbook, and update supplementary materials—which may or may not address the problem. In fact, so rarely does an updating of curriculum move the needle on student performance; when it does happen, it becomes a celebratory event.

More likely, it's the culture within the school—the relationship between teachers and students, the students' sense of emotional, intellectual, and physical safety, and the teacher's willingness and ability to personalize instruction for each student—that impacts student learning.

We know from John Hattie's work that the teacher is the single most important factor in student learning—but our focus in school improvement often remains on the curriculum.[1] Why is that? Likely, because it's easier to change curriculum than it is to change people. Schools have indicated a willingness to shift their thinking by changing from Directors of Curriculum to Directors of Instruction, an acknowledgment that it's the instruction, not the math book, that makes the greatest difference in student performance. But—regardless of the job title, much of the work remains focused on the content rather than the culture of the school, and as long as that remains the case, schools will continue to show minimal gains.

Recognize, also, that creating structures often provides a tangible result—a document with a plan laid out in black and white—whereas the effort to build culture may or may not provide immediate measurable impact. Because of the demand in our culture for "deliverables"—physical evidence of work completed—it's easy for leaders to get caught up in the belief that creating revised curriculum documents, organizational charts, and assessment templates is worthy of their focus when in fact, efforts to improve school culture will have a far greater—and longer-lasting—impact on school performance.

Theory in Action

The notion that a culture of trust is a necessary characteristic of high-performing schools is keenly understood by Muhammad Irshad Barkat, principal of the Middle School Beaconhouse School System Allama Iqbal Town Campus (BSS-AITC) in Punjab, Pakistan.[2] BSS-AITC is a private school serving students at all grade levels in the Lahore section of Pakistan's largest city.

When first joining the school as principal, Muhammad spent the first few weeks simply learning how the school operated. He visited classrooms, observed students and staff in the cafeteria, and watched as they followed their daily routines. During those observations, he started to form opinions about the school's strengths and areas of needed growth—but he kept those observations to himself and began thinking about how he might convince his teachers to share their opinions and ideas with him.

Muhammad quickly determined a need to engage and empower staff in authentic ways—a task that proved challenging at first. When asked for their concerns and ideas for improving the school, section heads and teachers initially withheld their thoughts, likely for two reasons: (1) their input had not been sought on a regular basis in prior years, and (2) Muhammad was a new leader who was unknown to the staff. Not knowing how Muhammad would respond to their suggestions, nor what he would do with the information they brought to the conversation, led teachers to remain largely silent in these early conversations.

Sensing the hesitancy of both veteran and newer staff members, it would have been easy for Muhammad to "fill the void"—a common mistake of inexperienced leaders. This occurs when leaders are uncomfortable with silence and impatient with hesitancy. Rather than remaining silent and providing opportunities for others to step forward, leaders who fill the void feel the need to swoop in and save the day, ending the silence with their own thoughts—an act that not only takes away the opportunity for others to speak but also injects the leader's opinion in the matter at hand, further stifling those who may not want to appear oppositional or draw the displeasure of leadership.

Muhammad chose a different approach, remaining silent except to offer an occasional prompt, giving others plenty of "wait time" as they considered a response. Most often, he reminded staff that they had the knowledge and experience that came from working at the school, and he did not; they had been there for decades in some cases, and he was brand new. He expressed that he needed their help to accurately define the challenges they were facing and the solutions that would lead to school improvement.

After what Muhammad described as a period of "disbelief and reluctance," a few of the braver souls among the staff began to offer ideas and suggestions for school improvement. As they spoke, Muhammad wrote down each thought without interruption, keeping a running record of the concerns and ideas. In some cases, their ideas led to deeper discussions and the implementation of a new strategy. In all cases, staff were made to feel that their voices were important and their ideas were worthy of consideration.

This strategy, with Muhammad demonstrating personal restraint and opening the floor for others at all levels of the organization, began a cultural shift at the school; staff members and teachers began to feel empowered to share their experiences and talk with one another—and with school leadership—about their ideas to address those concerns.

Once the conversations began, Muhammad understood it was incumbent upon him to ensure there was a follow-up discussion in which each idea was thoroughly vetted and explored. Once teachers saw that their ideas were given due consideration—sometimes even leading to the implementation of an approach they had championed—they understood that Muhammad was serious; he authentically valued their input and believed their experience mattered.

Later in the school year, Muhammad took it a step further, opening up his budget preparation files and asking teachers for their input about the allocation of resources, especially for professional development and innovative project development. This act—essentially putting his money where his mouth is—was well received by staff. They realized they were not only being listened to, but they were also being given access to what many teachers say is the least understood aspect of their school—budget development and the distribution of fiscal resources.

The results have been impressive. Within five years under Muhammad's leadership, the school was recognized as one of the top 100 schools in all of Pakistan, with an 87 percent academic success rating, earning prestigious British Council accreditation.

"The story is that of a success achieved purely on the basis of trust," said Muhammad. "I needed their help because they had been in that school for quite some time and had a far better understanding of the situation. At the same time, I assured them that I trusted their expertise and would fully support the ideas they proposed with all the resources they required."

Muhammad's approach exemplifies the principle shared in my first book, *The Trust Imperative* (2022), which is that we must first demonstrate trust in others if we are to expect them to begin to trust us. By empowering the staff to identify problems, suggest solutions, and have a voice in the allocation of resources to implement their ideas, Muhammad personified the empowering leader who fosters a culture of trust that permeates all levels of the organization.

Let's remain overseas for a moment and look at another example of a school leader who views culture as the single most important characteristic of a school's efficacy. Olamitoyosi ('Toyosi') Babatunde recognized early on in her role as Head of School for Pampers Private School in Lagos, Nigeria, that her participation as a colleague is vitally important to her staff.[3] "I do not believe in sending my people where I haven't been before," said 'Toyosi.

This is an important point to consider when thinking about school culture. I once served as the keynote speaker at a professional development day for several hundred staff members at a regional workshop day involving three local school districts. At the end of the presentation, several teachers approached me and said, "I appreciated what you had to say about school culture and trust; I just wish my administrators were here to hear it!"

This was a disappointing revelation. The organization had created a professional development day designed to address school culture—and several of the school leaders had skipped out on the workshop. It's unlikely they were doing anything unprofessional in their absence; the missing leaders were probably in their offices, cleaning up email and catching up on pressing matters. However, the message to their staff was loud and clear: "My work is more important than yours, and my time is more valuable than yours, so I'll be in my office while you participate in the educational opportunity that I scheduled for you."

This is a prime example of culture devouring structure. While the school leaders had created the structure for a meaningful growth opportunity—with teachers learning alongside those from other districts—they did more damage than good by not joining in. This became apparent in the breakout sessions that followed the keynote address, as teachers in the smaller setting expressed their frustration that the ideas shared in the keynote likely would not be adopted, since their leaders were absent. Although they were presented with various strategies for taking these ideas back to their schools, the teachers who were present struggled to get past the idea that their leaders had skipped out on something they were required to attend.

This is a simple concept: your participation as a leader is critical to the development of a collaborative, trusting culture. Participatory leadership is demonstrated by a compilation of simple gestures—from engaging in professional development opportunities to supervising the cafeteria, joining a student lesson, or picking up pieces of trash as you walk around the school. No task is beneath the school leader who strives to build a culture of trust, collaboration, and pride in the organization. When leaders believe they are above others, rather than alongside them, culture suffers.

In Lagos 'Toyosi takes this approach with employees at all layers of the school. "I believe that we cannot have an outstanding school if the non-academic team does not understand the vision of the school and their role in it," she says. "I see everyone as an invaluable member of the team."

The importance of having staff in all sectors of the organization fully committed to the school's mission cannot be overstated. Later, we will explore the idea that your most important job as a leader is to hire staff in every position—from bus drivers and custodians to guidance counselors and teachers—who are experts in their field, who care about kids, and who understand the mission and core values of the school. If you do that well, and then provide those expert staff members with a voice in how the school is operated and the resources to do it, your job will be much easier—and more enjoyable, too.

This is a concept 'Toyosi learned from her father, a civil engineer who shared stories with her of his willingness to listen to less educated but highly experienced construction workers on his team. He pointed out that many of his best ideas came about because he listened to what his team members had to say. "When an idea comes from a member of the team, I let everyone know who shared the idea," said 'Toyosi. "If we are attentive to issuing penalties when there is an infringement, then we must also be intentional in handing out applause for a job well done."

'Toyosi believes this approach has led to a freer expression of ideas and opinions among staff and students as well as parents. "Parents saw themselves as partners and referred to the school as 'our school' because their critiques and ideas were welcomed and taken into consideration," she said. "Many returned to the school or reached out years after to say how their children were helped and how well they were doing because of the solid foundation they had been given."

I was fortunate to learn this lesson early in my leadership career while attending a seminar at the Principals' Center at the Harvard Graduate School of Education (HGSE) in 2003. While there, we were privileged to hear from many leading researchers and practitioners in school leadership, and participants spent much of the week furiously scribbling down meaningful jewels of wisdom from each of them.

Two particular quotes stood out and solidified my approach to this work. One came from Prof. Richard Elmore, a longtime member of the HGSE faculty whose research challenged many school leaders to seek authentic improvement in student performance by paying attention to both the culture and the structures within the school.[4] Most notably, Elmore (who passed away in 2021) stated, "The process of improvement is fundamentally about changing the culture of schooling, and cultures change through face-to-face relationships."

One could argue that Elmore's statement is even more important today, as much of the communication in schools has devolved into shared docs, chat rooms, and text messages. While each of these tools may be used in specific situations to improve efficiency, they will never replace the benefits of school leaders engaging with others in person and developing meaningful relationships through authentic interaction.

Shortly after Elmore's address, we had the opportunity to hear from Dr. Pedro Noguera (currently the Dean of the Rossier School of Education at the University of Southern California)—yet another impressive researcher whose work has led to important school improvement efforts at schools all over the globe.[5] As a result of his research, Noguera challenged those of us at the seminar by stating, "You must change the culture of the school, not the organization of the school, as it is the most important feature of high-performing schools."

Noguera brings us full circle to Drucker's opening quote in this chapter. Whether it be corporate leadership in the mid-twentieth century or school leadership in the early twenty-first century, while structures certainly matter, those in positions of leadership must understand the critical importance of culture, first and foremost.

Creating a trust-filled school requires significant and intentional effort in two realms: structural and cultural. In the structural column are those protocols, procedures, and policies that define how the school is organized—how problems are identified and named, how input is sought, and how decisions are made. Structures that can be used to promote trust include items such as task forces and committees, employee handbooks, and well-defined workflow procedures. Each of these items gives form and function to the organization that promotes collaboration, communication, and coordination—all things that provide a sense of trust for employees.

However, structure without culture is a trust-crushing vacuum. A school may have all the right structures in place—task forces, focus groups, and standing committees designed to seek input and offer ideas for improvement—but if the culture is not one that fosters trust, these structural items are all for naught. In fact, structural items such as these that exist in an organization where the culture is poor often add insult to injury, as employees will ridicule and resent the false promises made by dismissive leadership.

School leaders who hang their hats on the structures they have created but fail to focus on their own interactions with others and their approach to the work will find that the best-intended structures only add to the frustration of employees as they see the disparity between how we *say* we operate and how we *do* operate as an organization.

With that in mind, we'll spend the next few chapters exploring how leaders build culture first and implement structures second because trust-building structures are more easily designed and implemented when a foundation of trust is present in the school. Cultural changes are more challenging and require greater thought and intentional effort by the leader. Only by fostering a culture of trust can leaders begin to authentically implement and adjust organizational structures that lead to school improvement.

For Thought and Discussion
1. Identify the structures in your school that, if implemented properly, promote a culture of trust.
2. Are the structures you identified being implemented as intended? What evidence exists to support your answer for each? If not, what needs to change?
3. If you noticed a drop in math scores for students in your school, how would you determine if the problem is the curriculum or the instruction? If the challenge is instruction, how do you address that in a trust-filled manner?

4. How do you attempt to impact culture in your school? Identify specific strategies you employ to create a culture of trust.

5. Identify something you might change about your practice after reading this chapter so that you might exhibit more trust in others and generate more trust in the school.

Notes

1 Hattie, J., *Visible Learning for Teachers: Maximizing Impact on Learning* (Oxfordshire: Routledge, 2012).
2 Barkat, Muhammad Irshad, Email message to author, August 26, 2024.
3 Babatunde, Olamitoyosi, Email message to author, August 16, 2024.
4 Elmore, R., "Building a New Structure for School Leadership," *Lecture presented at the Harvard Graduate School of Education's Principals Center* (Cambridge, MA, July 8, 2003).
5 Noguera, P., "Standards for What? Accountability for Whom?" *Lecture presented at the Harvard Graduate School of Education's Principals Center* (Cambridge, MA, July 9, 2003).

3 Approaches to Leadership

Despite the general understanding that trusted leadership is necessary for an organization to operate most efficiently and effectively, trust remains an elusive quality for many leaders; one that many employees say is missing in their organization.

According to the 2024 Edelman Trust Barometer—a global report exploring the level of trust in organizations and governments around the world—approximately 79 percent of employees in the United States and globally trust their employer.[1] While many might remember being excited to score a 79 on a final exam in organic chemistry during undergraduate school, it's not an overly impressive score when you consider that this means one in five employees does not trust their employer. A 2021 Gallup poll paints an even bleaker picture, with only 23 percent of employees expressing trust in their workplace leadership.[2]

Combine this finding with Zak's work on the impact of trusted work environments on the brain and performance mentioned in Chapter 1 (better attendance, higher engagement, greater productivity[3]), and it becomes clear that intentional effort to cultivate an authentically trust-filled work environment is critical to the health of any organization, let alone people-oriented workplaces such as schools.

While philosophers and academicians have theorized about leadership since the time of ancient civilizations in Greece, Rome, and Asia, it is really the past century during which specifically identified theories have been developed for consideration by aspiring leaders. Beginning with Thomas Carlyle's "Great Man Theory," which was developed in 1840 and popularized nearly 100 years later, researchers and theoreticians have attempted to identify the traits, characteristics, and actions of effective leadership and assign a descriptive label to promote their theory.

A quick search on the internet tells us that at least twenty different leadership theories or styles are currently being studied or promoted through a variety of professional learning organizations, summarized in Table 3.1.

It is unlikely that any leader's performance can be defined by just one of these theories. The overlap in definitions, the changing demands of the work, and the need to apply a range of approaches to varied challenges will result in a leader demonstrating traits of numerous theories in a specific situation.

Likewise, selecting one leadership style and adopting it for the duration of one's leadership career is impossible—and unnecessary. While it is both interesting and informative to understand various leadership theories, the study should be undertaken merely to open one's mind to the different possibilities that exist for improving one's approach, as it is your approach to leadership that will set you apart from others.

One's approach—or orientation—to leadership is to the general perspective from which one tends to address a challenge. Rather than spending time here rehashing well-developed leadership theories and attempting to recommend one over the other, let's look at how one approaches the work, for it is one's orientation toward leadership—which can be easily adjusted, as we will discuss later—that determines their effectiveness in most situations.

Over four decades of observing school leaders, I have found that they lean toward one of two overarching approaches to leadership. I call these two

Table 3.1 Leadership Theories

• Trait Leadership	• Behavioral Leadership
• Contingency Leadership	• Transactional Leadership
• Leader-Member Exchange	• Adaptive Leadership
• Servant Leadership	• Authentic Leadership
• Charismatic Leadership	• Ethical Leadership
• Participative Leadership	• Laissez-Faire Leadership
• Autocratic Leadership	• Democratic Leadership
• Situational Leadership	• Visionary Leadership
• Transformational Leadership	• Cross-Cultural Leadership

approaches *accountability orientation* and *empowerment orientation*, and from the titles themselves, you are probably already beginning to remember leaders you have observed that fit under one heading or the other. While we will take a closer look at each of these orientations throughout this chapter, it is helpful right at the start to look at a quick summary of what is meant by each.

In accountability-oriented organizations, the focus is on control and command, with nearly every decision based on compliance and policy. The accountability-oriented leader operates from the position that everyone in the organization *does* things *for* the organization to help the organization meet its goals, such as:

- Showing up on time
- Managing resources well
- Completing tasks as assigned
- Following policies and procedures as defined

This approach has been the dominant (no pun intended) approach to leadership for many decades. It is the style many are convinced exists in highly efficient organizations such as the military, financial organizations, and construction. In accountability-focused organizations, the leader's primary focus is ensuring that no one is breaking the rules, violating the contract, or wasting time and resources.

No doubt this is an approach that has produced meaningful results in many settings, and there is certainly something to be said for a school in which everyone is held accountable to one another, to their clients, and to the mission and core values of the organization.

To be clear, there's nothing wrong with a focus on accountability; in fact, accountability is critical for an organization. Without accountability, there are no standards to be met, no goals to be attained, and no norms to be followed. However, there is a case to be made for a better approach that leads to greater accountability without it being the sole focus of the leader, which leads us to empowerment-focused organizations.

For empowerment-oriented leaders, accountability is still important, but that accountability is cultivated by focusing not on what each employee *does for* the organization, but on what each employee *is given by* the organization, including:

- A voice in matters of importance to them
- The resources they need to do the job
- Opportunities to be innovative, take chances, and advance in the organization

From these quick summaries, it is clear to see the difference in the two approaches, and some might begin to infer that one is bad and the other good. We should avoid making that judgment too quickly. Rather, it might be better to consider each approach as being *effective*, but one has the potential to be *more effective*, helping a school meet both its aspirational goals and its accountability goals.

Accountability Leadership Orientation

Accountability has been an important part of school leadership since the beginning of public education, but it has never been more important than in today's world of high stakes testing and instantaneous access to school performance measures. From the publication of *A Nation at Risk* in the mid-1980s to the federal adoption of the No Child Left Behind Act in the early 2000s, the focus on accountability in US public schools has continually increased.[4]

The current political climate creates a pressure cooker for leaders who may have to place their school's state-determined letter grade on their marquee in front of the school or post student test scores on the district website. At the same time, national publications use snapshots of student performance data to rank schools, students and families go to social media to rate their teachers, and statewide data dashboards publicize student performance, staff qualifications, and a plethora of additional information about each school.

In this culture of formal and informal accountability, and a history of uplifting leaders who are decisive and forceful, it is no wonder many school leaders subscribe to accountability orientation. Like everything else subject to gravity, the pressure to produce good results flows downhill.

Throughout the country, we want our nation's schools to compare well with those in other countries, which leads to individual states wanting their schools to compare well with those in other states, which leads to local districts comparing themselves to others in their region. Unfortunately, these measures of accountability too often focus on standalone, standardized measures that do not consider the many factors that impact performance and are not true indicators of an individual school's effectiveness—but that is a book for another day.

Accountability leadership orientation is not necessarily an outgrowth of the focus on school accountability that has grown in the past four decades. In fact, the reverse is more likely the case; it is accountability-focused leadership at the highest levels of government that has led to the extensive accountability measures imposed on schools today. The result is a perpetual cycle in which school leaders are being held accountable with no say in the metrics to which they must answer. Therefore, they feel they must hold others accountable—and the cycle continues.

Leaders who adopt accountability leadership orientation identify their most important role as ensuring that everyone furthers the organization's mission by showing up on time, doing their job well, and using resources efficiently while following the policies and protocols set by the Board and administration. In their worst moments, accountability-oriented leaders rely on command-and-control strategies and are accused of being inflexible, black-and-white rule followers who lack empathy.

Before going much further, it is important to reiterate that accountability itself is not a bad thing. In fact, a school leader can enjoy a long and productive career—and have a positive impact on the performance of many students and staff members—working from an accountability orientation tempered with empathy and common sense. However, there's a better approach that fosters even deeper accountability while promoting growth, innovation, and higher performance.

Empowerment Leadership Orientation

When school leaders believe it is important to ensure each employee has a voice in matters that impact their work, the resources necessary to do their job well, and the opportunity to pilot innovative practices in a safe environment, teachers are empowered to innovate and suggest programming that best engages students. Just as accountability flows downhill, so does empowerment. Educators who are empowered to have a voice in matters of importance to them are more likely to empower students in the classroom (e.g., providing choice, group decision-making, and development of classroom norms), which leads to students taking greater responsibility for their own learning.

Research in private sector industries has shown that increased empowerment actually leads to increased accountability. This is likely because empowered employees feel a greater sense of ownership in the decisions that are made, therefore feeling more personal accountability than they do for decisions that are handed down to them. In other words, leaders who want to step up accountability in their organization are better off focusing on empowering employees—and students—than employing a command-and-control approach.

It takes a healthy level of authentic self-confidence and trust to assume an empowerment-oriented approach to leadership. Inviting input, allowing others to improve ideas with suggestions of their own, and providing consistent opportunities for others to innovate, experiment, and learn through trial and error are much more difficult than sticking strictly to well-defined policies and rules. It requires comfort with discomfort and calls for a leader to use judgment and discretion, rather than relying solely on language from the collective bargaining agreement, Board policy, or personnel handbooks.

Before exploring empowerment leadership orientation further, let's take a couple of minutes to discuss what it is *not*. Empowerment is not enablement, entitlement, or a laissez-faire approach to leadership. It requires a skilled leader to provide voice and choice to constituents without simply allowing everyone to do whatever they want without answering to the standards of the organization. That is enablement in its worst form, which happens when a leader relinquishes all authority and allows others to make decisions for which they have no accountability.

Entitlement happens when leaders allow others to assume they have a right to be treated differently than others around them. This occurs when leaders play favorites or uphold standards inconsistently. Constituents begin to believe that rules and protocols don't apply to them, taking empowerment to inappropriate levels. When constituents consistently operate as if they need not adhere to the norms and rules of the school, the structures and culture of the organization begin to break down, and mistrust is sown with other constituents.

Both entitlement and enablement occur when leaders adopt a laissez-faire approach to leadership in which they simply stop doing what they are supposed to do out of laziness, fear, or ignorance. Some may say there is a fine line between empowerment-oriented leadership and the laissez-faire approach, but there is a broad, bright line between the two, and leaders would do well to avoid crossing it.

The empowerment-oriented leader knows exactly what problems the organization is facing and is clear about the protocols and policies that are in place to guide each employee and student in their work. They are willing to push the envelope in encouraging constituents to share ideas, try new things, and propose innovative solutions. These leaders are fully engaged in collaboratively identifying problems and searching for solutions. They stand behind their employees when new strategies are being piloted, and they stand in front of their employees when criticism is being directed at the organization.

Conversely, the laissez-faire administrator is not engaged in identifying problems or searching for innovative solutions. While this style may empower others in the short run and provide them with opportunities to lead in individual situations, the leader's disengagement results in enablement, entitlement, and—most likely—power struggles throughout the organization as others attempt to fill the void left by an absent leader.

Empowerment-focused leaders demonstrate trust in their employees by ensuring that structures providing for employee voice are honored, decisions are made collaboratively—with authentic input from others—and employees are treated with compassion and empathy. This approach has gained traction in recent decades, not only in traditionally democratic institutions such as schools but also in private sector industries, where employee voices lead to greater buy-in of the organization's goals.

Ritz-Carlton Leadership Center, a consulting group born from one of the leading hoteliers in the world, has spent a great deal of time studying employee empowerment and accountability. Their findings indicate that empowered employees feel more accountable to the organization because they have had a say in the programs, structures, and policies that drive their work.[5] In other words, leaders who truly want their employees to feel accountable to the organization should employ the command-and-control approach to accountability less and the empowerment approach more.

Once that shift is made, employees will experience a greater voice in the policies, programs, and structures of the school. This will lead to greater engagement among teachers who are more vested in ensuring the successful creation and implementation of structures that matter. When this happens, Ritz Carlton found the real beneficiaries are the clients, who experience better service from the organization. Drawing the analogy to schools, the beneficiaries of an empowered organization will be our students, who will experience better instruction, programming, and care.

When leaders act with an Accountability Orientation, they ensure that everyone in the organization *does* certain things in certain ways at certain times. Conversely, when leaders act with an Empowerment Orientation, they ensure that everyone in the organization *has* certain things in a multitude of ways at various times.

Theory in Action

Dr. Michael Fitzpatrick is the longtime superintendent of the Blackstone Valley Vocational Regional School District in Upton, Massachusetts.[6] When Michael was named as the district's superintendent in 1993, significant reform was taking place throughout Massachusetts. One piece of legislation shifted the responsibility for hiring new teachers from the local school board to the principal and superintendent, and Michael was ready to empower his staff not only by providing them with a voice in the hiring process but also by publicly avowing to abide by their recommendations in all but the rarest of cases. "The rare exception to not advance a recommended candidate would only take place if I was aware of information the interview team was not," said Michael. "Thus we embarked on a partnership built upon trust."

In stating his intention—and following through on that intention—Michael made it clear that he valued staff input, and that he was a person of integrity who was willing to hold himself publicly accountable to his commitments. As staff came to feel trusted *by* him, they in turn came to put their trust *in* him, and the ensuing thirty years produced a long list of accomplishments that would have been far less likely without the foundation of trust that had been laid in the earliest days of Michael's tenure.

"By providing teachers with constant support for new ideas, the school has sparked enthusiasm and made system-wide improvement attainable," said Michael. Openness to new ideas has resulted in the development and implementation of strategies such as a longer school year, performance contracting, integrated academic and vocational-technical units, portfolio assessment, and staff-identified professional development.

As a result, enrollment at Blackstone Valley has doubled, the dropout rate is negligible, and standardized test scores have improved steadily. In addition, staff retention and student attendance rates are high because—as was postulated earlier—when staff (and students) feel empowered, they want to be present. "A willingness to incorporate team-suggested refinements increases ownership of the process and its products," Michael believes. "None of this would have been possible without a partnership of school leaders and educators built on a solid foundation of mutual trust."

When school leaders look to others in our industry—as you are doing by reading this book—we recognize there are thousands of current and former colleagues from whom we can learn. While the situations and dilemmas we face may be new to us, it is unlikely that they are new to everyone. Taking advantage of the vast experiences of those who have come before us or who are working alongside us simply makes sense. Pretending to have all the answers and ignoring the opportunity to learn from others is unnecessary in the field of education, where we are typically not truly in competition with one another anywhere other than in interscholastic endeavors.

However—learning only from others in education is a mistake too often promulgated by leadership development programs and professional development speakers. While seasoned educational leaders can offer us lessons specific to challenges at school, we should also embrace opportunities to learn from leaders in other fields—from business to government to the military—as we recognize that leadership is leadership, regardless of the setting.

Steve Smith is the Chief Executive Officer at L.L. Bean, one of the leading US-based providers of outdoor equipment and clothing in the world with annual revenue approaching $2 billion.[7] It employs approximately 1,000 people year-round, and an additional 4,000 during the holiday season, with stores in 20 states and offices on several continents.

As one enters Steve's office—located in Bean's warmly apportioned corporate office building—one cannot help but notice three words written on the top of the whiteboard positioned next to the large conference table in the center of the room:

"Empathy Transparency Integrity"

Steve wrote those words on the board when he first began his role at the company, and he left them there as a reminder to himself and others that they are the values by which he has attempted to lead various organizations for two decades. "I expect to be held accountable for leading with each of those," Steve said. "They provide a cultural guidepost for me and for the organization."

While empathy as a leadership quality has only recently begun to earn top billing alongside virtues and skills such as honesty, effective communication, and courage, it is something Steve has emphasized throughout his leadership career. "When you put a dilemma on the table, the more diverse perspectives you have trying to solve that dilemma, the better," Steve stated. "We ask, 'How will this decision be felt by (various constituents)?'"

One characteristic of leading with empathy is a willingness to accept that others' perspectives and experiences may be different from your own. This is a concept that was impressed upon Steve from his earliest days in the executive suite. "I had great mentors—including incredible female leaders—who instilled in me a curiosity about why someone thinks differently than me," Steve said.

Leading with empathy empowers others to share their perspectives more willingly, knowing that their opinions matter and their ideas will be given full consideration. When this is the case as a general practice, employees more easily accept those times when their proposals are not adopted, knowing that they will have other opportunities to express their opinions in matters of importance.

Adding to that empowerment is Steve's commitment to transparency. Aligning with the Ritz-Carlton research discussed earlier, Steve says, "You should share as much information as you can with your team; the more they know, the more they care."

One way Steve demonstrates transparency is through the "town hall" style employee meetings held at Bean's throughout the year. Rather than standing on a stage—with a podium or conference table separating him from the attendees, and the lighting set so the employees are in the dark and executives are in the light, Steve prefers to sit on a barstool on the ground level of the auditorium, with the house lights lit. Sitting with the employees, literally at their level, with no physical barrier between them and all able to see clearly, Steve and his team take visible action to build collegiality.

While these may seem like small details, the effect on those sitting in the audience is noticeable. Employees feel like they are part of the discussion rather than an audience being spoken to. The opportunity to ask questions, seek clarification, and offer suggestions furthers Steve's commitment to transparency and solidifies a sense of both empowerment and accountability for the employees.

Michael's work at Blackstone Valley and Steve's work at L.L. Bean, although being done in very different settings, illustrate the impact of empowerment-focused leadership. In each case, the employees are engaged because they are empowered to do so, and they feel accountable to the organization because they've had a say in decisions that matter. The contrast is clear; accountability-oriented leaders focus on what their employees *do*, while empowerment-focused leaders focus on what their employees *have*—ensuring that they have what they need to do the job well.

At the leadership level, empowerment comes in many different forms, and it is no less important. Building and department leaders want to know that they are empowered and trusted to lead their centers with a recognized level of autonomy while working within the parameters of the district. That empowerment begins at the leadership level, where the superintendent and school leaders work alongside one another to set the course for the district.

Thomas Giard, III is Superintendent of Schools in Waterford, Connecticut, where he leads the educational effort for 2,600 students in a public PreK-12 district.[8] Tom's work to build trust throughout the district begins with his work guiding the leadership team. "If trust exists amongst the leadership team members, and that is evident and visible to others, that permeates an organization," Tom said.

Two specific strategies have been particularly useful in building trust among leadership team members in Waterford: Pre-mortems and Red-teaming. "We did not invent these tools, but their use has been vitally important to building trust and getting better results," Tom adds.

While post-mortems have been common for many years in schools and other organizations to review events that have already occurred (albeit under different names, such as critical incident review, after-action review, or incident debrief), the pre-mortem is a lesser utilized approach in which the leadership team imagines that a project or initiative has gone wrong. The team then works backward from the point of failure to determine why things went wrong, and how the failure could have been prevented.

In Waterford, Tom led his team through a pre-mortem exercise during a summer leadership retreat. Each school principal shared a draft of their proposed school growth plan, and the team assumed the plan "failed spectacularly." The group then identified reasons why each plan failed and the themes that emerged from those reasons, which included:

- Too much, too fast
- Failing to clearly explain the why behind the initiative
- Lack of stakeholder input
- Not research-based

For a pre-mortem to be effective, the facilitator must effectively prompt participants to think about the reasons why a plan might fail, what has been overlooked, what assumptions have been made, and what can be done to promote success. Most importantly, the group must trust one another to be tough on issues, but gentle on colleagues. Nothing is gained if ideas are shared aggressively, dismissively, or with disdain.

Once the themes are identified, leaders can identify the tasks that will increase the plan's likelihood of success, along with who is going to be responsible for taking on those tasks and a timeline for completion. Leaving the pre-mortem with clear direction and specific steps to be taken is the first sign that the activity was worthwhile. Reduced rates of conflict, failure, and confusion throughout the organization are the longer-term indicators that will be revealed over time.

Whereas pre-mortems came out of the world of academia, promoted most notably through the *Harvard Business Review*, red-teaming is a process that first gained popularity in the US Department of Defense as far back as 1960.[9] In red-teaming, a group aggressively challenges their own proposal or concept, attempting to expose weaknesses they might otherwise overlook as a result of their own confirmation bias (which comes from developing the proposal with others who want to be convinced of its viability).

One example where Tom applied red-teaming was when Waterford's middle school administrators were preparing to communicate the school's move to standards-based grading. One group of school leaders acted as "adversaries" critiquing the administration's communications, staff presentations, faculty agendas, and research.

"Our goal was to challenge their thinking as a way to strengthen how they rolled this initiative out," said Tom. "This is more of a devil's advocate protocol meant to simulate stakeholder pushback they were likely to face from parents, staff, students, Board members, and maybe even me! In this instance, this exercise absolutely helped the administrative team of the school fine-tune their approach and messaging."

As with pre-mortems, a good deal of trust must exist in the room to produce impactful results. The assigned adversaries must be direct, yet thoughtful, even while playing the role of critics. The facilitator plays a key role in guiding the conversation toward fruitful discussions that address the greatest needs and lead to actionable items.

"These two types of exercises have been invaluable to our team in building trust and getting better results. It forced us to be vulnerable in a positive way and shed ourselves of the tunnel vision about our own work," said Tom.

The work of empowering leaders by creating a trusting environment with others throughout the district is critical for the empowerment of other staff members and, eventually, students. When empowerment (but *not* entitlement or enablement) is pervasive—your school will operate more effectively and serve students in ways that cannot occur in a command-and-control environment.

Doing the Work

To nurture empowerment in your school, consider a few simple strategies:

Seek Input

Opportunities abound for school leaders to invite faculty voice in areas of importance to them, including the academic calendar and schedules, curriculum mapping, professional development topics and programming, review of staff and student handbooks, and hiring teams.

A word of caution: Offering these opportunities may sound enticing—but if you fail to define how the input will be used, or you set aside the input altogether, you will actually degrade trust in the organization rather than build it, as mentioned in Chapter 2. Approach this work with your eyes wide open; know where it is that you value faculty/staff voice, so you can authentically provide opportunities that will honor the input received.

Seek Feedback

Many leaders take the brave step to ask for input on their own performance on a regular basis, including in formal, anonymous surveys of leadership at least twice per year. Providing opportunities for constituents to share their perspectives on your leadership performance is an important and necessary step toward developing humility, vulnerability, and empathy. In Chapter 15, we'll look at one model for doing this.

Encourage Innovation

Create a safe environment for staff to offer ideas and try new approaches, and provide candid feedback aimed at improving opportunities for students. Leaders who authentically value input from staff welcome their thoughts on a range of topics and avoid shutting down conversations with hypercritical, degrading, or dismissive comments.

Demonstrate Curiosity

Many leaders—especially those in the early stages of their career or those who feel challenged in the role—feel it is their role to provide answers and solutions in every situation. Of course, as fallible human beings, we want to be seen as intelligent and confident by our constituents, and we too often enter the arena—or the meeting—determined to provide the answers as proof of our leadership skills and knowledge.

A more effective, collaborative strategy is to approach each situation from a position of curiosity. Rather than entering a meeting ready to propose your ideas, try scripting out a few questions you have on the topic at hand. Chances are these questions will spur dialogue and reduce the feeling that others are there to adopt your solutions. Recognize that the best thinking typically comes through shared decision-making, rather than from a single individual. Your idea may be a good one—and it might be improved when others have a chance to discuss it openly.

Trust First, Then Seek to Be Trusted

Finally—start each day from a position of trust. The vast majority of educators want to do their best for students; those who don't will come on your radar soon enough, and you'll then have an opportunity to grow trust in your leadership through firm, empathetic, and graceful redirection. If we don't trust staff, we end up micromanaging every situation, wasting our own time and energy, and disempowering those around us.

When school leaders bemoan—or brag—about 60-, 70-, or 80-hour work weeks, it seems apparent that they are not efficient, not effective, and do not trust and empower their staff to do the work they've been hired to do. This is no way to lead a school; the job is too big for one person to control every decision, and we must engage and trust others if we are to do the job well.

Failing to empower others could leave your school stuck in an accountability rut, where a focus on test scores and timecards leads to a stale curriculum, undervalued teachers, and unmotivated students. Empowering others will make your job easier and promote student engagement in learning that matters.

For Thought and Discussion
1. How important is accountability in your organization? What are the things students and educators are accountable for?
2. How might greater empowerment raise the level of accountability for (a) staff and (b) students at your school? In other words, if an individual student or staff member felt more empowered, how might that increase their feelings of accountability to the school?
3. What steps could you take to increase empowerment for staff and students at your school? Identify specific, concrete actions you can take within the next thirty days to empower others at your school?

4. How much pressure do you place on yourself to identify solutions? Do you demonstrate curiosity and draw out the perspectives of others, or do you dominate airtime during meetings? At your next meeting, try to be intentional about demonstrating curiosity and letting others speak.

5. How will you invite and honor staff input in meaningful ways?

Notes

1 "2024 Edelman Trust Barometer," *The Edleman Group* (November 24, 2024), https://www.edelman.com/sites/g/files/aatuss191/files/2024-02/2024%20Edelman%20Trust%20Barometer%20Global%20Report_FINAL.pdf.
2 Ratanjee, V., "How to Build Trust in the Workplace," Gallup (June 14, 2022), https://www.gallup.com/workplace/393401/trust-decline-rebuild.aspx.
3 Zak, P. J., *Trust Factor: The Science of Creating High-Performance Companies* (New York: AMACOM, 2017).
4 Gardner, D. P., *A Nation at Risk: The Imperative for Educational Reform. An Open Letter to the American People. A Report to the Nation and the Secretary of Education*, National Commission on Excellence in Education (ED) (Washington, DC, April 1983), https://eric.ed.gov/?id=ED226006.
5 Aveling, G., *The Ritz-Carlton Experience: It's All in the Implementation* (July 2009), http://www.brandingasia.com/columns/017.htm.
6 Fitzpatrick, Michael, Email to the author, August 3, 2024.
7 Smith, Steve, Personal interview, November 18, 2024.
8 Giard, Thomas, Email to the author, July 30, 2024.
9 Klien, G., "Performing a Project Pre-mortem," *Harvard Business Review* (2007), https://hbr.org/2007/09/performing-a-project-premortem.

4 Mission-Driven Trust

One of the initial steps an organization must take on its journey to being highly efficient and effective is to develop and consistently implement a concise, commonly understood mission statement. Add to this a well-defined set of core values, and the organization will have laid the foundation for a sustained effort toward common goals and expectations.

The highest performing organizations—whether in the private or the public sector—are consistently found to have a clearly communicated, collaboratively developed mission statement, along with a set of well-defined core values that drive their day-to-day operations and interactions. These statements clarify the organization's purpose, reduce conflict, identify priorities, and enable leadership and staff to focus their energies on practices aligned with the mission. Consider these samples from the world of business:

- "Our mission is to entertain, inform, and inspire people from around the globe through the power of unparalleled storytelling."—Disney
- "Our mission is to empower every person and every organization on the planet to achieve more."—Microsoft
- "Our mission is to strengthen the financial well-being of our customers and deliver better outcomes for the clients and businesses we serve."—Fidelity

Each of these provides us with an example from a multibillion-dollar corporation, each with a global impact in their respective sectors of the market. Despite the complexity of their work, each organization's mission statement is relatively short, easy to understand, and memorable to employees who will be tasked with meeting it. This is a critical characteristic of an effective mission statement; it is manageable, understandable, and—best of all—memorable.

Even better, these statements can be marketed in a way that is even more relatable to the staff and clients. For example, Microsoft claims to be "Empowering Others," while Disney proclaims itself "The Happiest Place on Earth," to simplify the mission and make it known to anyone who encounters their organization.

Adopting a mission statement that attempts to describe every goal and action in the organization is almost as useless as having no mission statement at all. Schools with multi-sentence, multi-paragraph, or even multi-page statements are not uncommon—and the likely result is a mission statement that sits on a shelf, forgotten, and dismissed even by those who helped to develop it.

When discussing the importance of a succinct mission statement for schools, I am often asked if each school within the district should have its own mission statement and separate set of core values. Before answering that question, think about the size and complexity of the organizations used as exemplars above. Given that these multibillion-dollar, global corporations operate each with a single mission statement, why would a local school district, even the largest one in the country, need multiple mission statements to define its work? When we adopt that approach, we are complicating the work and creating silos within the district.

A better approach is to ascend to the proverbial 20,000-foot view for your district and define what it is that you are really about and what you aspire to provide for your students. Articulate it in one sentence, then market it, make it actionable, and live it. While living the mission may look different in a PreK classroom than it does in an advanced physics classroom, the mission itself should be consistent throughout every program, curriculum, and activity in the school.

Early in my leadership career, this was a deficit in my thinking. I felt the development of the organization's mission statement demanded too much time and energy from staff. We were all educators; was it not clear what our mission should be? However, as my own leadership has evolved, and as I have experienced different levels of buy-in and collegiality in various districts, I have come to believe in the power of a strong, clear mission statement that has been developed with thoughtful input and communicated with consistency. Today, I view it as one of the most critical foundational steps in building trust in an organization.

My thinking has evolved on this topic because of several significant experiences. The first of these was the result of a charge given to me by the school board in my first year as a superintendent of schools. My first day on the job was also the first day for the new school district, which had been formed by the union of two separate districts in response to a new state law that required their consolidation. There was a great deal of acrimony leading up to the formation of the larger district, as one can imagine when several communities with different identities, traditions, and tax bases were forced to unify under one organizational umbrella.

Significant differences in collective bargaining agreements—and thus, employee salaries and benefits—were just one example of the differences that would challenge our efforts. Varied states of facilities maintenance, different priorities in updating curriculum, disparate levels of funding for schools, and incongruous investments in important items such as classroom technology, communications platforms, and professional development all contributed to a clear sense of unrest and distrust among the communities.

Wisely, upon hiring their new superintendent, the Board stated that one of the first challenges would be to engage the community in the development of a strategic plan, which should include a mission statement that would be used to unify the district and drive our decision-making in a common direction.

Prior to this work, my experience related to mission statements was limited to the adoption of internal, school-based mission statements that were created by the faculty in response to an expectation from the school's accrediting agency. This work was typically completed over several meetings of the staff and resulted in a wordy, cliché-filled statement that was recorded in the accreditation report and quickly forgotten as the day-to-day demands of running a school dominated our attention.

In this new district, though, with Board members who were experienced leaders of private and public sector organizations, the work began with engaging the community along with the staff. As will be discussed in Chapters 12–14 (Strategic Planning), surveys, forums, and focus groups were used to engage constituents, and the goal of developing a meaningful and memorable mission statement was soon attained.

The work leading to the adoption of a district mission statement and the unity that resulted from people coming together to craft that mission marks the earliest moment when my thinking began to change. If the work of developing a mission statement could bring people together—some of whom didn't want to be together—and lead us to a common understanding of what we were trying to accomplish, then how much more effective might it be in organizations where there is already some agreement as to their purpose?

With our new mission statement in hand—as well as our freshly developed list of core values—we began the work of developing consistency and equity at all levels of the organization. From curriculum updates to major facilities renovations, and from collective bargaining adjustments to student technology decisions, the district began moving forward together for the betterment of all schools. This is not to say that all disputes were resolved; there was still plenty of opportunity for outside forces to derail our work, but within the schools and with the support of many in the community, clarity of purpose and a reduction in disputes provided for a more harmonious balance and a focus on improving student outcomes.

The second major impact on my thinking as a mission-focused leader was when I left that district and became the superintendent of a district that had historically valued the importance of a well-developed, clearly stated mission due to decades of effective leadership. The district had an outstanding reputation throughout the region. By all traditional and anecdotal measures, the district was considered a high-performer, and the teachers and administrators themselves were considered not only excellent educators within their schools but leaders among their peers in other districts.

As with my first superintendency, when hired in this new district the knowledgeable Board members once again charged me with overseeing the development of a new strategic plan. The difference between this task and the work undertaken in the previous district was that this new district had been in its current configuration for several decades, had adopted a concise, impactful mission statement and set of core values more than ten years prior, and was actively promoting that mission on its website, letterhead, and throughout the schools.

It became apparent early on in our review of the mission statement that there was no need for significant change. The statement had served the district well for more than a decade; people knew it, could recite it, and could locate it if it needed to be referenced. There had been at least some mention of the mission at various meetings and presentations each year, and though it should not be overstated to indicate that the mission was driving decision-making, it certainly provided an umbrella under which most decisions could be harbored.

This preexisting inclination toward acknowledgment of the mission and core values of the district made it easy from my earliest days as the superintendent to take its prominence in our schools to a higher level. As will be discussed later in this chapter, the strategies for increasing awareness of the mission and core values—among staff, students, and families—are many and varied. They all drive us toward a common goal, with common language and common values, thereby reducing confusion and conflict and providing a foundation upon which all decisions can be made, all behaviors addressed, and all outcomes focused.

The final experience that solidified my belief that a widely accepted and understood mission statement is critical for building a trust-filled school that performs at its highest possible level came when I started teaching graduate courses to aspiring school leaders. The vast majority of students were practicing educators in a variety of roles—mostly classroom teachers, but also counselors, social workers, paraprofessionals, and other support personnel.

Because I had come to believe in the importance of mission-focused school culture, one of the assignments students were asked to complete each semester involved a quick exploration of their school's mission. They were asked to locate the mission statement and interview three colleagues and three students about the mission and its prominence in decision-making, goal-setting, and student-teacher interactions at the school.

For the most part, the papers turned in each semester reflected a discouraging trend. Consistently, approximately 50 percent of students either could not find any mission statement for their school, or they found it only after asking someone who was able to locate it in a document filed somewhere in the school office or library. The mission statement, if one existed, did not have any impact on operations and interactions at the school. Nobody interviewed knew there was a mission statement, much less what it said or how it impacted their daily work.

Of the remaining half of the students, most could readily locate a mission statement for their school. It was posted in classrooms and on the school's website, and colleagues could point to a time or two at the start of the school year when it was mentioned in a staff meeting. Beyond that, it was not a major focus of their work, and students were unaware that it existed.

Each semester, there were a handful of students—sometimes only one or two, who proudly shared that their school's mission was clearly and consistently communicated in a variety of ways. These educators claimed that their school's mission and core values impacted decisions on a daily basis, as these statements and beliefs were promoted, honored, and modeled by the school's leadership consistently and effectively.

Even more impressive at these schools were their students' responses to the interview questions. Especially at the higher grades, but even among elementary grades in some settings, students reiterated their teachers' claims, easily identifying the school's mission and core values and assuring the interviewer that the statements were, indeed, embodied by their teachers and created a culture of learning for the school.

After assigning this exploration for several semesters, a noticeable trend began to appear. It became very clear that those who reported little to no use or promotion of their school's mission and core values consistently worked in schools that were struggling to meet student needs, performing poorly by most traditional measures, and often in turmoil at the leadership level. These graduate students felt stifled by the lack of direction in their schools and were motivated to become school leaders themselves because of their frustration with the existing leadership.

Meanwhile, the schools in which the staff and students were well-versed in the mission and core values were schools that had stellar reputations— not just because of their student performance on standardized tests, but because they might also have a particular focus—a mission that met the unique student needs in their setting. The graduate students who worked in these schools wrote with pride and enthusiasm about their schools and their leadership. They were motivated to become school leaders because they had seen it done well, and they believed it to be a rewarding and impactful profession.

It was this third experience that most notably pushed me to improve my own leadership by ensuring that our schools are mission-focused, with a clearly communicated set of core values that drive our planning and decision-making. It is no coincidence that schools with a clear mission and core values also have outstanding reputations—often because they provide students with innovative programming, plentiful opportunities for student voice, and appropriately rigorous instruction. They are less often in turmoil, as their mission and core values provide a north star that reduces conflict and provides for quicker resolutions when conflict does appear.

Promoting the Mission

The first step toward living your mission as a school is to promote that mission in very public ways. From the moment anyone interacts with your school, they should understand your mission. Whether they access your website, receive communication by email or hard copy, or apply for a job at any level in the organization, people should be introduced to your mission in a visible way.

Publicizing Widely

Look at your school's website and social media applications. If your mission—or the tagline that represents your mission—is more than one click away from the landing page, it's too far. Your mission needs to be front and center on all your digital channels. This is an easy fix as a first step toward promoting your mission in a tangible manner. Similarly, your core values or beliefs about learning should be easily accessible—just a click or two away from your landing page, with meaningful definitions that allow the reader to know exactly what you mean by each value.

These definitions help you promote the values you most want exhibited in your schools. If you can't decide between "Integrity" and "Honesty" as you attempt to narrow your list of core values to a reasonable number, select one and use the other as part of your definition. Honesty is one component of integrity, just as compassion is one component of empathy and patience is one component of perseverance. You don't need to list every positive quality you hope to embody—be selective and use definitions to touch upon a broader array of positive characteristics.

Likewise, students, staff, and visitors to your school should be introduced to the mission and core values as they walk through the building. Posters, murals, and various displays should bombard anyone walking through the school's corridors or sitting in an office or classroom, and everything that goes up on the walls should be an indicator of a school that is working to attain its mission.

Hiring with Intent

The application and interview process for new hires offers another opportunity to declare your mission and core values before a new employee starts working at your school. While placing your mission at the top of your job application is good, including a statement about your school's mission and core values is even better—and including a question about your mission is best of all. For example, consider a school with a mission slogan of "Empowering, inspiring, and engaging." You might ask your applicants to select one of the words from that slogan and write about why that word resonates for them, and how they see themselves embodying that characteristic in their work at your school.

That's a strong message, right from the start, that your school places great emphasis on its mission. Applicants will get a sense that you mean what you say, and that you are leading a mission-driven organization. When you follow this up with a related interview question or two, the candidates get an even deeper sense of the school's commitment to its mission.

Due to the cyclical nature of the academic calendar, there are many opportunities each year to promote the school's mission and core values, and it is incumbent upon school leaders to seize those opportunities. Once you have your mission emblazoned on each of your digital and print media and posted throughout your schools, you can tackle the next step, which is promoting your mission through presentations and training.

The first opportunity each year will likely be the onboarding process for new hires. During this orientation phase, new staff members are likely to learn about a variety of topics that are germane to their work; network logins, security protocols, curriculum expectations, and so on; there's a lot to learn as new employees join our schools. This is also a critical time to orient them to the mission and core values of the school, and it should not be left to anyone other than the school leader to make that introduction.

Your school-based or district-wide onboarding program provides the superintendent or principal with a prime opportunity for communicating how critical the mission is to the work of the school. It should be important enough that the new employees hear directly from the CEO of the organization, "This is who we are, this is what we stand for, and this is what we are about." I have found that such a message resonates with employees in a powerful way.

Even years later, employees often remark that being introduced to the mission in a meaningful way right as they started their work made them feel like they were part of something special; that's one effect we want this work to have.

Buy-in and clarity are essential if staff are to model our core values each day. In just a few interactions with your district—from the application process, through the interview process, and now in the orientation process, new employees have had at least three touchpoints with the school's mission statement, and they've now had the head of the organization share with them how important it is that they understand and align themselves with the core values.

Kicking Off

Typically, as summer vacation draws to a close, superintendents and principals send out their welcome-back letters to staff and families, highlighting important dates and exciting changes for the upcoming school year. This is another opportunity that should not be missed when you consider how to center your district's work on the school's mission.

This doesn't need to be a lengthy descriptor of the mission or a complete listing of the school's core values, although that may be a nice touch. Simple statements inserted into the annual letter serve as subtle reminders that yours is a mission-driven organization, as shown by the examples below:

- *"In keeping with our mission to prepare each student for their brightest future … "*
- *"Concentrating our efforts to empower all students to lead fulfilling lives … "*
- *"As we seek to inspire students to lifelong learning … "*

We know modeling is one of the most effective forms of leadership. Speaking about your mission in simple ways and continuing to use that language in communications throughout each school year will encourage others to do the same.

Many districts hold opening ceremonies at some point during the professional in-service days at the beginning of the school year, providing another opportunity for school leaders to highlight the school's commitment to its mission. Displaying the mission throughout the facility where this ceremony is being held—projected onto a screen at the front of the auditorium or meeting space as well as on any handouts—helps to embed the district's commitment in each employee's mind from the first day of school in the fall.

During the welcome ceremony, school leaders should use a bit of data, share a couple of celebrations, and apply some self-deprecating humor to highlight the mission and one or two core values of the school. You want this opening ceremony to energize and inspire the staff; optimism matters, and sending them off to their classrooms, offices, and school buses on a high note, with a sense of purpose and unity, is critical to your school's culture.

Engaging the staff in the presentation is another strategy that has been employed to encourage buy-in to the district's mission. Asking for volunteers to share what each of the district's core values means to them—or how they see the mission statement impacting their work with students—can be an effective way to keep the audience's attention focused on their own role in furthering the goals of the school.

One district leader has gone so far as to purchase some "mission swag" for their employees. As each teacher, custodian, counselor, bus driver, or other personnel entered the auditorium for the opening ceremony, they were offered a T-shirt with the school's logo and mission emblazoned on the front. Not only were staff pleased to receive this simple gift, but they were also proud to wear them at various points throughout the year on special occasions—like Homecoming Week, Dress Down Fridays, and other celebrations of school unity.

Mission Moment

All of this focus at the start of the school year is commendable, but we all know what happens once the students arrive in the fall. School leaders and staff step onto the running wheel and spend the next ten months trying to keep pace with all the activities around them. How do we keep the focus on our mission and core values when we're doing all we can to keep our heads above water, with student discipline, curriculum revision, budget development, and analysis of student assessments bearing down on us each day?

One strategy to consider is to hold a "Mission Moment" at the start of every staff meeting. During this moment—which may run as long as five minutes or slightly longer—staff engage in a simple activity designed to help them remain grounded in the unifying work of their school's mission and core values.

The Mission Moment may involve watching a video, observing an image, reading an article, or responding to a prompt that in some way ties to their mission. A brief discussion—in small groups or as a whole staff—provides an opportunity for each participant to reflect on their role in promoting the organization's work.

The Mission Moment also serves as a way to step out of the hustle and bustle of the school year and refocus on your overall purpose. The brevity of the moment recognizes that there is much work to be done, many decisions to be made, and many tasks to be completed; you want to be efficient with your time while providing a few minutes of reflection when possible. A balance must be maintained between reflection and task completion, or the staff will begin to resent the time taken to reflect.

District leadership should serve as an effective model by holding a Mission Moment at the start of each district-level team meeting. School-based leaders can then replicate the activity provided at the district meeting in their own school-based staff meetings, further creating a sense of unity and commonality among all educators in the district.

Student Discussions and Discipline Management

Imagine stepping into the lobby of a middle school located anywhere in the world just before the start of the school day. You approach a group of students socializing in the school's lobby. After greeting the group, you ask them, "Can you tell me what the core values of your school are?"

Several of the students excitedly say, "Yes!" and they begin to rattle off a quick list of the school's values.

You ask, "How do you know about these core values?"

One student replies, "Well, they're on posters all around the school, and we talk about them during our advisory almost every day."

Another student chimes in,

Yeah—and I got in trouble for throwing a piece of my blueberry muffin at one of my friends in the cafeteria during lunch, and when I got sent to the office, the assistant principal asked me if I could tell her which of the core values I had violated, and how I was going to repair the harm I had done.

This is a school operating on a different plane than most. When students know, accept, and buy into the core values of the school, opportunities are created that allow educators to interact with students and their families in more engaging and focused ways.

One of the most effective ways to learn about a topic is to teach it to others, further embedding the concepts in one's own mind. In this same vein, expecting educators to spend time on a regular basis discussing the school's mission and core values with students promotes buy-in and commitment not only with the students but also with the staff who are leading the discussions.

At the elementary level, many schools have "morning meeting" or "home base" activities at the start of each day. This provides an excellent setting for discussing the school's core values and what they mean to elementary students. Elementary teachers have unique opportunities to instill in their students a sense of belonging and unity and to begin using a common language that will be reinforced throughout their students' time in the district.

At middle schools and high schools, a daily "advisory period" or "homeroom" provides ongoing opportunities for mission-focused discussions. These few moments offer another opportunity to bring the school's core values into focus.

It is highly likely that teachers are already having these discussions in one manner or another, but those discussions may be disjointed from one classroom or one grade level to the next, as teachers espouse the virtues of kindness, patience, and sharing in individually developed lessons. Standardizing the language and focusing on these lessons through promotion of the school's core values give every student in the school a similar understanding of the school's goals and expectations.

This is not to say that every one of these daily meetings should be dominated by exploring the school's mission statement, but once or twice a week by design and other times as the opportunity presents itself, discussion of the school's core values should occur with students.

To promote this work at each school, grade-level teams or building leadership teams should create a year-long plan reinforcing the mission and core values in appropriate terms for their students. As with all things, some teachers will embrace this work with excitement, while others will need to be encouraged more deliberately. Providing teachers with core materials and suggestions for facilitating the discussions will make it much more likely that they will embark on the work with enthusiasm. Engage those who wish to be leaders in this effort, and they will provide their colleagues with an endless list of ideas for mission-focused student activities.

The example given earlier of the student who threw the blueberry muffin at their friend provides another sampling of how the school's mission and core values can be reinforced with students. It is likely that every misbehavior that occurs in school will violate one or more of the school's core values. Teachers and administrators should be prepared to begin disciplinary and restorative conversations by asking the student to identify the core values their actions violated. Taking this approach once again promotes a common understanding of the school's mission and core values—instilling those values in the student and in the staff member serving as the interventionist.

Decision-Making

Making use of the school's mission and core values is critical during decision-making moments. Whether the decision being made pertains to budget priorities, program expansion, reduction in force, educator effectiveness, or any number of important subjects that come across the school leader's desk each day, a focus on the school's mission clarifies the decision to be made and reduces the likelihood of conflict. When deliberating, school leaders are encouraged to consider two questions that will assist in this effort:

- How will this decision further our school's mission?
- Which of our core values will be promoted by this decision? (Or, which of our core values could be violated by this decision?)

This sounds great in theory, but it can be difficult to envision in the practical setting of a leadership team meeting; I often provide the example of a decision we had to make during my first year as a superintendent of a district that had recently become a one-to-one technology device district for students in grades 3–12. The school's mission had been simplified to a three-word statement—"empowering all students"—and the community was struggling with a policy that was not aligned with the mission, largely because the mission was not being used to inform decision-making in the district.

Every student in the district had been provided either an iPad (grades 3–5) or a laptop (grades 6–12) for academic purposes. Because the school leaders were worried about theft, loss, and damage to these devices, they had imposed a rule that barred students from taking their laptops on school-sponsored trips. Whether students were attending a field trip, participating in an athletic contest, or performing in a musical production—regardless of how many hours were spent traveling to and from the event or how late they returned home in the evening—they were required to leave their devices behind.

This policy caused a great deal of concern for students—who just wanted to get a jump start on their homework, parents—who just wanted to pick up their children back at school without having to wait for them to go into the building to get their device, and staff members—who didn't enjoy having to unlock the school and wait for students to retrieve their devices after a late night trip.

As we discussed this policy and the problems it was causing, our Director of Technology, who had been present at the time when the rule was first implemented, spoke up to the group of principals and central office administrators in the room and said, "I guess if our mission is to empower students, we ought to trust them to take the school-issued devices on school-sponsored trips."

The policy was changed immediately—with a few reminders to students, parents, and staff members about proper care and security of the devices. Over the next year, we continued to track theft, loss, and damage to the devices, and were pleasantly surprised to see that numbers decreased in all three categories. By living our mission and empowering the students, they responded in kind by taking good care of their devices.

This tangible example of decision-making with the organization's mission in mind is repeated consistently in mission-driven schools and organizations. Whatever your mission is, keeping it at the forefront of your discussion will lead to a more intentional decision-making process at all layers of the organization.

A third question that should be considered when making decisions through the lens of your school's mission is one that focuses on equity for all students:

- "How will this decision impact Systemically Non-Dominant (SND) students?"

Answering this question, schools become more deliberate in their effort to ensure equitable practices and opportunities for all students. Jenkins provides an extensive list of SND characteristics of which school leaders should be aware.[1] By asking this third question, school leaders open themselves to further education and understanding of who their SND students and staff members are, and how existing and proposed policies and practices impact them differently from members of systemically dominant groups.

When speaking with groups of school leaders—as well as when teaching graduate students—I am frequently asked if I believe you can have a good school without all this focus on mission and core values. The answer to that question is, "Yes. However, I don't believe you can have your *best* school without a collaboratively developed, clearly stated, well-publicized mission in place."

Experience has proven—time and time again—that those schools that have been deliberate in their development and use of a simple mission statement, along with a clearly defined set of core values, are performing at higher levels than similar schools that are operating without those items. Mission-focused schools are driven toward continual improvement, regardless of their past performance or student demographics.

These may be high-performing schools by all the traditional measures, yet they are not resting on the laurels of standardized test scores or college-going rates. They may be schools with a well-defined focus serving high-need populations. In either case, they do not leave the understanding of a common mission to chance. They deliberately and intentionally use their mission and core values to further improve opportunities for students.

Leadership Modeling

One of the most important characteristics of a mission-driven school is the public commitment made to the mission and core values by the leadership team. Without leadership buy-in, the mission will most certainly fade into the background and the school will be less likely to move forward with consistency and reduced conflict. When leadership dedicates itself to the mission in thoughtful and meaningful ways, others in the schools will be likely to follow suit, leading to a cohesive approach to problem-solving and program development.

Dr. Jacqueline Coe, Superintendent of School Administrative Union 24 in Henniker, New Hampshire, understands the need for clarity and commitment to the mission at the leadership level, which she believes is enhanced by adopting commitment statements that drive the work for her team. "The commitments are the beliefs and practices that we engage in as leaders in the district. They underpin our work and influence all aspects of decision-making," said Jacqueline.

Jacqueline and her team have invested professional development time reading the likes of Stephen Covey, Simon Sinek, Brene Brown, and others before settling on a list of core beliefs on which they all agreed:

- All people can learn
- Each person deserves to belong in our schools
- It is essential to have a shared why
- Clear is kind and unclear is unkind (from Brene Brown)

The team then identified the guiding principles by which they would lead the district:

- Decisions are stronger when those impacted are involved
- A PreK-12 approach better supports the whole child
- We assume the best intentions in our interactions
- Our students are best served when we engage their families
- Trust is foundational and we seek to build it
- We reflect on and learn from each experience
- Our decisions are grounded in evidence, process, and/or policy
- We are responsible for creating structures and processes that empower people

Similar to the importance of a collaboratively developed, well-communicated mission and set of core values for the organization as a whole, these statements are vital in setting clear expectations for the leadership team in their work together on behalf of the organization. Jacqueline says, "By explicitly articulating the practices that we are committed to and sharing those with the wider community, we are welcoming accountability for the practices."

When the school community sees a visible commitment to the organization's mission by leaders throughout the district, they will be more willing to be accountable to the mission themselves. Strong ties between leadership commitments and the school's core values provide a consistency of focus that promotes greater collaboration and a collective effort to make the mission a reality.

Mission Inventory

As you consider where your school stands regarding its focus on a commonly known and understood mission, you might consider surveying your staff, or at least your leadership team, using the Mission Inventory provided in Table 4.1. Your score on this self-assessment will provide you with an indicator of the work to be done to become a mission-driven school.

By asking others to share their perspectives and scores on the Mission Inventory, you gain an understanding of where your school could improve in this area. If your total score is from 0 to 3, you are at square one, and the planning process described in Chapters 12–14 may be most helpful as you embark on the determination of your mission and core values.

If your total score is between 4 and 10, you likely have a mission statement that can be found somewhere. You should consider dusting it off and determining if it still applies, or if times have changed so significantly since it was adopted that you should move back to square one and begin the process all over again. If the mission still seems applicable, you will want to lean into reminding others of its existence and determining how best to publicize and promote the mission to drive your work.

Schools scoring 11–14 are likely well ahead of the field in their awareness and use of the mission statement. For these schools, a focus on continual improvement will lead to the adoption of strategies like those identified throughout this chapter to ensure the mission is being promoted in all possible locations and is being used to drive decision-making processes at the school.

You will know you are becoming a mission-driven organization when you start to hear educators outside of your leadership team talking about the mission and core values in meaningful ways; you'll know the work is becoming ingrained throughout all levels of the organization when you hear

Table 4.1 Mission Inventory

1. If asked, each staff member in my school could easily recite our school's mission statement and/or core values.			
0 Not at all	1 Not likely	2 likely	3 Absolutely
2. If asked, most students in my school could easily recite our school's mission statement and/or core values.			
0 Highly doubtful	1 Not likely	2 Likely	3 Absolutely
3. Our mission is prominently displayed in every learning/meeting space in our school.			
0 Not at all	1 Somewhat true	2 Likely	3 Very much so
4. Our mission is a primary component of our digital presence (website/social media, etc.)			
0 Not at all	1 Rarely	2 Consistently	3 Constantly
5. Our mission and core values are a major focus of our professional development and onboarding activities and our school-wide presentations and communication.			
0 Not at all	1 Rarely	2 Consistently	3 Constantly
6. We have a systematic way to ensure that every decision in our schools is made through the lens of our mission and core values.			
0 Not at all	1 Rarely	2 Consistently	3 Constantly
			TOTAL: _____

After answering all six questions, total up your scores and find where you fall on the index:
15–18: Mission-driven
11–14: Mission-informed
8–10: Mission-aware
4–7: Mission-deprived
0–3: Missionless

parents speaking to the mission in focus groups, public forums, or private conversations; and you'll know the work is having its most important impact when students speak to the ways in which they and their teachers embody the core values on a daily basis.

Every school should strive to be mission-driven. The development and implementation of a common set of expectations and goals provide a culture of unity and collaboration that offers each school opportunities for improvement. Without it, we are leaving to chance the shared understanding and vision of where we are headed and how best to get there.

For Thought and Discussion
1. Without looking it up, write down your organization's mission—or at least the slogan or tagline that represents your organization's mission. Is it memorable and meaningful? Were you able to recall it without difficulty? Do you think others who work or learn in your school would be able to do so?
2. Take a look at your school's website. How easy is it to find the mission statement and core values? Are there other digital opportunities for better promoting these statements?
3. Where else is your mission promoted (letterhead, business cards, email signatures, agendas, etc.)? Are there missed opportunities in this regard that you could correct immediately?
4. Complete the Mission Inventory in Figure 4.1 and ask others to do the same. How do your answers differ from one another? Where are their consistent deficiencies, and how might those deficiencies be improved?

5. Do you believe a greater focus on your mission and core values will reduce conflict, provide clarity, and build greater trust in your organization? If so, what steps are you willing to take to make the mission more commonly known among staff, students, and the community?

Note

1   Jenkins, D., "IST of an ISM: Systemically Dominant and Systemically Non-Dominant," *Share the Flame* (2025), https://www.shareflame.com/.

5 Authentic Visibility

Like many superintendents, Dr. Joseph Baeta held several leadership positions in various schools before becoming superintendent of the 3,500-student Stoughton Public School District in his hometown of Stoughton, Massachusetts.[1] The challenges faced in those earlier roles led Joe to develop a visible style of leadership that he refers to as the "Three Vs of Educational Leadership":

- Visibility with students;
- Visibility with staff; and
- Visibility with the school community.

Joe's understanding of this need was initially fostered while he was serving as a high school principal, where he came to realize how meaningful his presence was to constituents in and around the school. As he attended school events, visited classrooms, and greeted students and staff each morning, Joe said, "I started to see how my visibility was scoring 'points' with staff, students, and the school community. I wondered why, and it was such a simple answer: I was part of them."

While his initial efforts stemmed from an intentional strategy for coming to know the school during the transition process, Joe made the decision at that early point in his leadership career that he must maintain visibility through direct contact with colleagues, employees, students, and families. Thus, he began an intentional effort to serve as a visible leader, a steady and constant presence in the corridors, classrooms, offices, and performance venues throughout the district.

"It requires authentic visibility. You are at the game on Friday night because you want to be there, not because you must be there," says Joe. "The best compliment I have received in 33 years was when a parent said, 'Thank you for taking the time to support my family while you are away from yours.'"

Authentic visibility is not just being seen—but being seen doing things that matter, interacting in meaningful and sincere ways that further the school's mission, engaging with staff, interacting with students, and experiencing the school day or after-school activity as others do. That type of authenticity takes deliberate effort and a strong sense of who you are as a leader and the type of organization you'd like to lead.

There are many challenges to being visible in meaningful ways. Certainly, the demands of the day often get in the way. Arriving at the office, you likely will have received dozens of new emails since you logged off the previous afternoon or, more likely, evening. With several meetings stacked up for the morning, you could easily get sidetracked from greeting students and staff as they arrive at school, instead taking advantage of a few unscheduled minutes to sign off on some purchase orders or approve field trip requests. While those tasks are important, they can also be completed at times when high visibility is less possible.

Highly visible leaders capitalize on opportunities to build trust in themselves and in the organization in a variety of ways, through inspiring practices that build cohesiveness among constituents. "I am not checking up—although every once in a while, that does happen—I am just checking in," said Joe. "It allows for me to engage in small talk and provides for trust to be both earned and granted."

In Chapter 4 we explored the importance of leadership focused on a collaboratively developed mission statement and set of core values. In this chapter, we go one step further by discussing specific steps school leaders should take to increase their own visibility so they may understand how staff and students experience the mission of the school on a daily basis.

Leaders who prioritize visibility model to others throughout the school that they are part of the team, that "we're in this together," and that they choose to prioritize people and relationships over policies and procedures. In this way they are modeling for others the importance of collaboration and their willingness to be a participant leader, as described by Toyosi Babatunde in Chapter 2. They are better able to understand the challenges faced by their colleagues and students, and more likely to engage in conversations with a wider range of constituents on a broader variety of issues than they would by remaining in their office.

Theory in Action

Jeff Rodman is the Executive Director of the New England League of Middle Schools (NELMS), an organization in Georgetown, Massachusetts, that provides professional development, schoolwide assessment, and student leadership opportunities that promote best practices in middle-level education.[2] Prior to serving in this role, Jeff was a middle school principal in several highly regarded school districts, including at the Middle School of the Kennebunks (MSK), an International Baccalaureate school in Kennebunk, Maine.

As with all school principals, there were many demands on Jeff's time during the school day. There is no doubt he could have filled his day without leaving the main office, but he chose a different approach, maximizing his visibility with students, staff, and families from the start of the school day right through to dismissal time.

Each day, Jeff looked forward to standing in front of the school or in the large, main lobby as staff and students arrived for the academic day. He was observed on many occasions, speaking words of encouragement to students who were preparing for a concert or a competition, congratulating those who had performed the night before, or sharing words of kindness and laughter with anyone walking past. One sensed that Jeff took as much pleasure from these interactions as he gave to those on the receiving end, with the message clearly being, "I'm here for *you*."

Even more impressive than his commitment to start the day this way was Jeff's mid-day routine, which was to be present in the cafeteria during each of the three lunch settings for the school. Throughout this nearly hour-and-one-half time period, Jeff would sit at tables with students, share a few moments with duty teachers, and thank the kitchen staff for their work. His presence signaled to teachers that he recognized the commitment it took to supervise the cafeteria and that it did not need to be a tortuous chore, and his low-key approach with students let them know that the lunch period was a time to relax and enjoy one another's company.

To top it off, as the students finished their meal, they were invited to step outside and enjoy time on the playing fields around the school—and Jeff, once again, joined them for the activity. Whether kicking a soccer ball, sitting on a nearby bench, or walking around the fields, he created a culture in which students knew he cared about them and enjoyed being with them; something not all school leaders convey.

As a result of this effort to be visible, the culture at MSK was one in which teachers felt supported and empowered, and where students felt seen and appreciated.

The power of Jeff's modeling was evident when teachers chose to eat in the cafeteria—surrounded by students—rather than alone in their classrooms or as a group in the staff room. It was also evidenced when teachers requested to begin holding a schoolwide wellness walk—with all students and staff—each Friday afternoon. And it was further evidenced when every teacher in the school stood on the sidewalk on the last day of school and waved goodbye to the students each spring, hollering, "We'll miss you! Have a great summer!"

While it may be an oversimplification to say that the culture of Jeff's school was collegial, collaborative, and student-centered just because he greeted students in the lobby each morning and ate lunch with them in the afternoon, it is not a stretch to say that the visibility he provided through his actions went a long way toward nurturing that culture. Any effort school leaders can make to be out and about with students and to take on duties that teachers may view with hesitancy will be met with appreciation by staff and students alike.

Visibility to students and staff can be a challenging concept for superintendents, whose offices may not be in or near a specific school. It can be even more challenging in extremely large districts where the superintendent oversees dozens of schools.

Dr. Curtis Finch, Jr. is the Superintendent of Schools for the Deer Valley Unified School District in Phoenix, Arizona—a district serving 34,000 students in 42 schools spread out over 362 square miles.[3] After twenty-six years as a superintendent—and a total of thirty-two years in school leadership positions, Curtis sees the call for visibility as an important one.

"Leading by example trumps anything you say," says Curtis. "I believe the building principal is the single most important leader in your school. If you believe in servant leadership, then you need to model it for your principals. How can a superintendent model this same approach? Being present in the buildings and classrooms was my answer."

To that end, Curtis pledged to his leadership team of 150 administrators during his first year at Deer Valley that he would visit 500 classrooms each year. Eight years after making that pledge, Curtis confirmed that he met the goal each year.

"At first it freaked the teachers out because they had never seen a superintendent in their classroom before, but now they appreciate and expect it," Curtis states. "The biggest impact has been on our culture. I have been able to get in front of problems earlier. Since 'culture eats strategy for breakfast,' you better be where the culture is built—in the classrooms (if you hope to make a significant difference in your schools)."

In order to pull off this gigantic challenge, Curtis schedules the school visits as part of his annual calendar. "If you don't plan your year well, you will end up not making it to the finish line," said Curtis. "The moral of the story is to schedule it. I keep a log of the schools that I visit in my car. By keeping track, I can make sure I get to all the corners of the district."

The call for greater transparency from leaders is a common refrain today—and it has been for decades. While it is important to be a visible leader so you can hear from others as you visit schools and classrooms, one of the lesser-talked-about benefits of high-visibility leadership is the opportunity for you to communicate your message to others in informal settings—which typically provides for more give-and-take and allows for varying perspectives, especially with leaders who create a safe culture for respectful dissension.

In Deer Valley, Curtis says, "By visiting the schools, I have been able to give the 'street view' observations of their campuses directly to (the principals) and reinforce what is important from my perspective and how it applies to their buildings."

This reinforcement and consistency of messaging from leadership are critical regardless of the size of the school or district. Countless times in my career working in districts of 1,500 to 3,500 students, conversations with building principals have revealed either an inconsistency of practice or an opportunity for collaboration that we did not previously know existed. By being visible, the leader also becomes more knowledgeable and serves as a conduit of information between schools, programs, and classrooms.

As the Head of School at KIS-Bangkok, Dr. Carolyn Mason Parker leads an International Baccalaureate school serving 850 students from more than

50 nationalities in Thailand's capital city.[4] During the 2023 school year, KIS leadership implemented a multifaceted approach to build trust in the school, with leadership visibility being one of the significant focal points.

"We committed to spending more time in classrooms and common areas," said Carolyn. "Leaders regularly participated in classroom activities, not only observing but also interacting with students and teachers, further reinforcing their presence and commitment to the school community."

The impact within the school was noticeable to staff and students alike. "The leadership's presence in the classroom—and their willingness to act on our feedback—has made a significant difference. We feel heard and supported," said one staff member. A student chimed in, "It's great to see our principal and vice-principals around the school more often. It makes us feel like they genuinely care about our experience and well-being."

Every school leader I have spoken with has indicated an understanding of the importance of greater visibility. Yet, in every graduate course I have taught, a consistent refrain is heard from students who are current employees in schools across the country: they don't see their school leaders living up to this expectation. Instead, they claim they rarely see their principal, they never see their superintendent, and non-evaluative administrator visits to classrooms are almost non-existent.

This begs two questions:

- Why is it that many teachers say they only see their school leaders on an infrequent basis, despite the universal belief that the most effective school leaders are highly visible in classrooms, corridors, and at events throughout and beyond the school day?
- How can school leaders change this perception and increase their visibility within the school and community?

The answer to the first question may be quite simple. While school leaders recognize the importance of seeing what is happening in their schools and thereby being seen in return, they are swamped with the multitude of responsibilities that fill their calendars each day. While they have every intention of visiting schools and classrooms, emails, phone calls, and meetings demand their immediate attention. If they get into one school for fifteen minutes and visit three classrooms, they feel good about it—but how much did it really impact their visibility on a large-scale basis? In a school of

150 employees, if 6 people saw the superintendent or the principal during 1 visit, a large majority could still say, "I never see my school leader," even though the leader can say, "I got into three classrooms today!"

In that regard, it's a problem of perspective. While everyone agrees that visibility is important, it's virtually impossible for school leaders to be visible to everyone due to the isolated nature of classrooms, the wide variances of staff schedules, and the demands of the job. The solution—and the answer to the second question—is to maximize opportunities for visibility in authentic, meaningful ways that provide tie-ins with other aspects of the work. The following examples have worked in various settings—for both school-based and district-level leaders—and can easily be modified and scaled to increase authentic visibility for leaders at all levels.

Doing the Work

Walking Meetings

One method that has proven successful for getting into classrooms and other spaces throughout the school is to schedule monthly supervisory meetings between the superintendent and each school-based administrator as walking meetings. This is a practice I began with our building principals several years ago in a deliberate effort to increase leadership visibility without increasing workload or having to set aside other items on our calendars.

Walking through the school while conducting business, we are able to accomplish two tasks at once, covering items of importance and maintaining leadership visibility. Rather than meeting behind closed doors in each administrator's office, we take time each month to walk through the school, popping into classrooms and interacting with students and staff. In a forty- to sixty-minute time period, a walking meeting can take us through an entire building, with stops in eight to twelve classrooms or more if the visits are brief.

Of course, if the building administrator has a confidential or sensitive matter to discuss, we spend a few minutes in their office, as that is always an option available to us, but for the most part, we can discuss the topics of the day while walking through the school. Meanwhile, the side benefit of getting some steps in and being more physically active is an added benefit.

All Hands on Deck

If your district was not experiencing a shortage of substitute teachers prior to the Covid-19 pandemic, it will likely do so at some point in the coming decade as people find remote work or more lucrative in-person opportunities in an economy that is starving for workers. Schools have a hard time keeping up with the salary increases and variety of employment opportunities that are drawing workers away from even the steadiest of substitute teaching positions. This leaves your district short-handed, and the teachers who are at work are often doing double duty, giving up planning periods, or teaching multiple classes at once to keep students engaged.

Like many situations in which employees are stressed, school leaders can build a great deal of trust by increasing their visibility when substitutes are in short supply. Even if it is for a small portion of the day—when the school administrator jumps into a classroom or duty period to help with supervision or instruction, students and staff take notice.

Shortly after the Covid-19 pandemic subsided and schools returned to in-person learning, I was contacted by one of our elementary principals who wanted to take me up on my offer to help out when they were shorthanded. "Can you cover recess duty for us?" he asked. I readily agreed, thinking I would enjoy stepping away from the office and getting some fresh air while watching the students play on the playground not far from my office.

When I arrived at the school to escort the students to recess, I was greeted by several teachers who were going to be my recess duty colleagues. As I approached, they were each calling out the areas of the playground they would cover. "I'll take the swings and monkey bars," said one. "I'll cover the soccer field," said another. After all but one area was covered, one of the teachers said, "Dr. Dolloff, can you cover the Gaga pit?" To which I responded, "Sure thing!"

Unbeknownst to me at that time, "Gaga pit" appears to be a civilized term for "Fourth Grade Cage Match." In the Gaga pit, students play a form of dodgeball, but with one ball and many bodies in an enclosed octagon, where they punch or strike the ball in an attempt to knock others out of the game by hitting them below the knees. It is the definition of controlled chaos.

Under my close supervision, the game became a melee within the first few minutes of the period, and I found myself futilely attempting to encourage fair play, sportsmanship, and controlled aggression for the full twenty-minute recess. It was exhausting and, despite my honest effort, the students clearly sensed that they were the ones in charge as this rookie supervisor knew neither the lingo nor the strategies for reigning things in.

As we walked from the playground back into the school, the teachers were sharing a good laugh as I told them I realized I had been played when they all staked their claims to the less intense playground pieces without clueing me in on the challenges of the Gaga pit. The pleasure they got from watching the superintendent attempt to control two dozen elementary students engaged in a high-intensity playground activity was surely one of the highlights of their year.

When we can have fun with students and staff, increase our own vulnerability a bit, and take on a task that we ask them to do each day, we create collegiality and nurture trust.

Instructional Engagement

Another great example of this approach comes from my father, a high school educator who served the same community from 1958 to 1994. For the final 26 years of his career, he was the principal of a high school of approximately 750 students on the coast of Maine. For several of those years, he spent one week each year teaching each ninth-grade math class at the school. As a former math teacher, he enjoyed staying in touch with both the subject matter and the art of teaching. More importantly, this gave him great visibility with students as they entered the school during their first year.

The connections that were made between the principal and students seemed to be much more meaningful than is typically found in schools. Rather than only coming to know the students who are best at grabbing your attention—for reasons good or bad—he came to know each of them in a small way through a week of classroom interactions, allowing him to know most students from the time they entered the school until the day of their graduation.

Of course, the impact on staff was significant, too. A principal who can teach? And who wants to do so? Again, taking on tasks that you ask your staff to perform, and modeling that you can do it well, is a powerful way to build a trusting culture in leadership.

The demands of the principalship and superintendency have changed, and it is unlikely that current school leaders could devote the kind of time to teaching courses that my father did in decades past. However, the concept is a solid one and worthy of consideration in some form or other. Any time you can make connections with students will restore your faith that your work is worthwhile and reaffirm your commitment to the profession.

Making Connections

Dr. Tom Farrell provides another example of authentic visibility with students. Tom served as a superintendent in Colorado, Maine, and Taiwan for more than three decades. At each of his stops, he searched for meaningful opportunities to engage with students. One such strategy led him to form a "Captain's Club" where he would teach a leadership course to students who were serving as captains of various sports teams or in leadership roles with student groups.

In one format, Tom would meet with these students once each week for the equivalent of one academic class period, leading discussions and activities designed to increase student leadership capacity. Students were invited to share ideas they were interested in promoting as leaders in the school, while also studying the challenges faced by leaders in the political, military, and business world.

Models exist similar to this all the way down to the elementary level, where one school principal Kelli Rogers provided first-grade students with the opportunity to participate in the school's "Captain's Crew" on a rotating basis. Each week, different students from first-grade classrooms were invited to meet with Mrs. Rogers and discuss ideas they had for improving the school. They then developed proposals and plans for bringing the ideas to fruition—or they learned to handle disappointment if their ideas were ultimately turned aside. From requests for swimming pools on the playground to pets in each classroom, the students learned how to formulate and share ideas and plans—and they did so while coming to know their school principal in an authentic and engaging setting.

Reviewing these examples of authentic visibility, it is clear that the most effective school leaders are intentional and creative in finding ways to engage with students and staff. The challenges of the work demand that school leaders plan, schedule, and commit to high-visibility strategies on a regular—if not daily—basis.

It may be teaching a class once a week throughout the school year, advising a student club or activity on a regular basis, or speaking with student groups or classrooms. The opportunities to be creative in this regard are endless, and school leaders who engage students in authentic ways will reap the benefits of meaningful interactions with students and collegial relationships with staff.

For Thought and Discussion
1. How do you "check in" without making it seem as though you are "checking up" on employees? What kind of follow-up do you provide after interacting with staff?
2. Identify the most meaningful ways in which you have interacted with students in your current leadership position. How often does this occur?
3. What are the benefits of greater visibility by school leadership? How does this visibility impact teachers, students, and families?
4. Identify leaders you have worked with who best personified authentic visibility. How were they able to do this, and what were the benefits from your perspective?
5. After reading this chapter, what new ideas have you considered for engaging staff, students, families, or the community through increased visibility?

Notes

1. Baeta, Joseph, Email to author, September 16, 2024.
2. Rodman, Jeff, Email to author, February 12, 2025.
3. Finch, Curtis, Email to author, August 6, 2024.
4. Mason Parker, Carolyn, Email to author, August 12, 2024.

6 Planning for Transition or Renewal

Whether you are a veteran who has been in your current leadership position for more than a decade or a newly hired school leader anticipating your first day on the job, taking time to review data, make observations, and hear from constituents is important if you are to understand the current challenges, anticipated demands, and changing nature of the school. While transition planning for new leaders is not a new concept, it can be that a similar approach, called renewal planning, should be taken by veteran leaders who want to recenter their focus and ensure they are providing the leadership the school and community need. The examples shared here can be used to formulate either type of plan.

If you recently accepted a new position as a school leader, congratulations. The work upon which you are about to embark is meaningful to the students, staff, and families of your community—and your influence will not end there. Education provides the foundation of a free democracy. While we don't often think about—nor receive credit for—the role our educational system plays in providing opportunity, promoting equity, and encouraging the pursuit of meaningful endeavors, rest assured that the work you do as a school leader is part of a larger network that provides a framework for the structures of a free and advancing society.

That's a pretty big concept to wrap your head around. The good news is that you aren't responsible for upholding the entire structure of our democracy. Still, the part you play locally goes a long way toward shaping the experiences and perspectives of citizens who are now or will soon be making decisions—as voters, educators, and elected officials—that will impact schools in the coming decades. Your challenge will be to provide every student with high-quality, personalized experiences each day so they will not only reach their greatest potential but also develop a sense of trust in our schools that will generate ongoing support throughout their lives,

To get off on the right foot as a new leader or determine if you need to refocus your work as a veteran, intentional work is needed. We'll begin our exploration of this idea by looking at a school leader of more than two decades who has learned through his experiences that the most important part of this work is the ability to gain insight from others.

Theory in Action

Kevin Estes is the Chief Academic Officer for the Ballard County School District in Barlow, Kentucky.[1] Earlier in his career, Kevin served as the principal of James T. Alton Middle School in Vine Grove, Kentucky, where he first implemented a transition plan that became a model for his progression from building leader to central office administrator.

Kevin's plan began with a thoughtfully written introduction to the staff and community, briefly expressing his gratitude for being offered the position and sharing his aspirational hope for the school. After this quick note of thanks, Kevin immediately stated his intention to seek input from a wide range of constituents as he focused his work on getting to know the school and community. His introduction was not full of "I" statements and did not provide the reader with a lengthy resume listing his personal honors and accomplishments. Rather, his letter contained several "we" statements, referencing the potential they all shared as a community, the vision they would develop together, and the journey they would take to make that vision a reality.

This humble approach sets the stage for collaborative leadership. People can go elsewhere to learn about Kevin's history; in this introduction, he simply wanted to express his excitement for the work and extend an invitation to be part of his transition to the school. This approach also works well for a veteran seeking input from the school community as part of a renewal plan. In that case, the community will already know who you are, so a brief description of your renewal plan should be enough to engage them in the process.

Goals and Objectives

To provide clarity of purpose, Kevin next chose to share what it was he hoped to accomplish through the execution of the transition plan. Four to six well-crafted statements are typically enough to highlight the focus of this work. While Kevin's statements were more specific to his school, it is helpful to look at abbreviated samples to further your thinking in this area:

1. Establish and nurture positive and productive relationships
2. Identify strengths and opportunities for growth for the school and community
3. Collaboratively develop a clear vision for systemic continuous improvement
4. Identify the strengths and areas for growth in curriculum and instruction
5. Identify targeted areas for growth with parent and community involvement

For veterans developing a renewal plan, the goals may look a bit different, though the focus should remain on fostering relationships, identifying strengths and weaknesses, and continuous improvement. Of course, without stating it, an underlying goal of all this work is to nurture greater trust between the school community and the school leader. While developing that trust is critical for a new leader, re-establishing that trust can provide a significant boost for the leader looking to energize the school community in a positive way.

Core Beliefs—A Personal Credo

In this section, Kevin identified his key values as a school leader. This may also be seen as a personal credo—those beliefs or goals that will guide his work.

Developing a credo is an exercise I assign to graduate students at the beginning of their first course in educational leadership. Although they have yet to spend much time learning about the challenges of school leadership, students rarely suffer from writer's block when asked to share their beliefs about how schools should be led. Like most employees, they've had enough experience observing their current leader to generate a lengthy list of how they believe they would perform if they assumed the role.

The value of developing your own personal credo is demonstrated during challenging times. Keeping a copy nearby—posted on your bulletin board or sitting in the top drawer of your desk—provides you with a visible reminder of what you stand for as you face the demands of the job.

Whether working with aspiring school leaders or those with decades of experience, challenging them to create their own credo and encouraging them to keep it nearby as a frequent reminder of their commitments is an activity that grows in value. While they may not appreciate the activity when they first go through the exercise, the experience becomes more valuable when they find themselves struggling with an ethical dilemma or a challenging situation at work, and they see that credo hanging on their wall or sitting on their desk, and their path forward becomes a bit clearer.

The following example of a personal credo starts with an opening belief statement followed by a list of core values—each with a defining phrase and examples of how those core values will be lived. Finally, the credo ends with a statement of how success will be measured—something many leave out when stating their beliefs. Amazingly enough, with the right prompts, this statement was largely created by Claude AI, then edited to suit the individual style of the administrator for whom it was created:

> *I believe that education is the most powerful catalyst for individual transformation and societal progress. As a school leader, my fundamental commitment is to create an environment where every student can discover their potential, develop their unique talents, and build the knowledge and character needed to become engaged, compassionate, critical-thinking citizens.*

My core principles are:

1 *Individuality: I recognize that each child is a unique individual with inherent dignity, extraordinary potential, and the right to learn in a supportive, respectful environment. No student will be marginalized or overlooked on my watch.*

2 *Equity: I am dedicated to dismantling systemic barriers and creating educational opportunities that are genuinely accessible to all students, regardless of their background, economic circumstances, or learning differences.*

3 *Collaboration: Education is not something done to students, but a collaborative process involving students, educators, families, and the broader community. I will foster partnerships that support holistic student development.*

4 *Continuous Growth: Learning is a lifelong process. I commit to cultivating a culture of continuous improvement for both students and staff, where curiosity is celebrated, mistakes are seen as learning opportunities and professional development is ongoing.*

5 *Empathy: Academic rigor and emotional intelligence are not competing values but complementary ones. I will lead with empathy and the understanding that academic success is deeply connected to students' social-emotional well-being.*

6 *Transparency: I pledge to lead with integrity, making decisions that prioritize student welfare, communicate openly, and model the highest ethical standards for our entire school community.*

7 *Innovation with Purpose: While respecting educational traditions, I embrace innovative practices and technologies that can enhance learning, preparing students for a rapidly changing world without losing sight of fundamental human connections.*

My ultimate measure of success will not be test scores or rankings, but the confidence, curiosity, and character of the young people who pass through our school. I will work tirelessly to ensure every student leaves our institution not only academically prepared but also inspired to make a positive difference in the world.

One can see how this credo can be used to drive decision-making and responses to critical situations for the school leader. Much like the mission statement that drives the work of the school district, a well-crafted personal credo provides the school leader with a visible, living document to which they can turn when times get tough and resolve is weakened.

My own credo was challenged when one of our children violated a team training rule during his senior year in high school. As a former coach, athletic director, and high school principal, I expected students to abide by the behavioral expectations we had of them or be subject to disciplinary consequences appropriate to the violation. I had long been a believer that we could—and should—hold student-athletes to higher expectations due to the privileged nature of interscholastic athletics.

As a result of those convictions, I had occasionally been on the opposite side of the table from parents who would turn a blind eye or, worse, deny the truth when their child violated the school's policies. Now I was faced with a personal dilemma, as my own child had violated the rules while in our own home, with nobody else around—seemingly providing us with the option of dealing with the behavior internally and preserving his participation in the athletic season.

We went to bed that evening not knowing entirely what we would do, but as I lay there, confused and disappointed, my wife asked, "What would you want any other parent to do?" In essence, she was asking me to consider the credo by which I had led schools and organizations for nearly two decades.

I knew at that moment that there was no question what our next steps should be. When we awoke the next morning, I told my son we needed to go to the school and have him tell his coach and athletic director what he had done. When he at first argued against this approach, I defended my position, saying, "When the season started, you gave your word that you would not do these things; now you need to tell them you broke your promise, and you'll have to deal with the consequences."

While that approach cost my son his captaincy and two weeks of games, we both look back now—more than ten years later—and recognize the importance of the stance we took at that moment. He recovered from the suspension and finished the season with grace, which taught him a valuable lesson about honoring your word. For myself, as the superintendent of a nearby school district, I slept better at night knowing that I had acted with integrity—even though I was tempted not to.

Your personal credo matters not only when it is convenient, but also when you are facing a difficult dilemma. Whether you are starting a new position or rededicating yourself to the work at any stage in your career, defining what it is that you stand for brings clarity to your effort and gives purpose to your tasks.

Kevin's credo included things like:

- Perception is reality
- Every student deserves our best every day
- Decisions will be made through a collaborative process based on what's best for students

Concise statements like those can bolster one's confidence and resolve in turbulent times. Listing them in your transition or renewal plan affirms for yourself and anyone who will see the plan that you have defined the standards by which you will live and oversee the school. Putting your credo in writing is the first step toward holding yourself accountable to the highest expectations you have for yourself and the school.

Timeline

The next portion of Kevin's plan included a timetable, broken down into three phases:

- Listening & Learning
- Listening, Learning, & Leading
- Leading & Progress Monitoring

Like many new leaders, Kevin's first day on the job came just after the end of the school year, providing him with more than two months to implement the first phase of his plan. This phase was designed to provide him with multiple listening and learning opportunities. He broke the plan down as shown in Table 6.1.

Table 6.1 Phase One: Listening & Learning

Action	Timeline
Meet with the outgoing principal and/or administrative team to discuss past instructional initiatives and future instructional needs of the school	Early July
Meet with the Superintendent and district administration to communicate the entry plan	Early July
Meet with administrative staff (asst. principals, guidance counselors, etc.) to review data, identify trends, and develop priorities for school-wide instructional practices	Mid-July
Invite each staff member to a 1:1 meeting • Instructional aides • Classroom teachers • Office staff	July–early August
Collaborate with administrative staff to plan opening day activities	July–early August

Depending on the job and the size of the organization you are leading, the list of interviewees to be invited to one-to-one meetings will vary greatly. While building principals will want to extend the invitation to every staff member, superintendents would do well to gather a sampling of staff members who are representative of their school, grade-level, learning area, or division.

Interviews should have a well-defined format, with a predetermined set of questions to be used as a guide for the conversations, allowing for some variance in how each conversation unfolds. Because you should be intent on building positive relationships, it may be wise to allow a conversation to wander into areas of commonality as well as areas of curiosity as you strive to know your staff on a deeper level.

Kevin set out to ask each staff member five probing questions:

1. Name three things at our school you *do not* want to see changed or eliminated.
2. Name three things at our school you think we *should consider* changing or eliminating.
3. When you first heard I was going to be the new principal, what did you think, "I certainly hope that he *does* ... what?"
4. About what did you think, "I certainly hope that he *doesn't* ... what?"
5. What other general advice do you have for me?

One can see how these questions can generate discussion beyond the responses offered. Your curiosity in fleshing out each response will be critical to understanding the perspectives of those being interviewed—an important step to take when leading with empathy.

One important consideration you will want to decide upon prior to the interviews is how you will record the responses. While various technologies exist for recording your conversations, there's something inherently suspect when you ask someone, "Do you mind if I record our conversation?" A less intense option is the old-fashioned pad and paper, which provides you with a summary of the ideas shared without making the interviewee feel as though they are being deposed.

Kelley Ridings, former superintendent of Shanghai SMIC Private School in Shanghai, China, took this approach as he assumed the reins of a school that had seen significant staff turnover in the preceding years.[2] "I took careful notes," said Kelley. "My attention to the conversation helped me later as I had information to refer to, and it also showed each staff member that I was listening."

Kelley's effort during the transition period created a sense of trust that proved beneficial later in his tenure. "I find that staff want to be heard and valued. Whether their viewpoint dominates in the end isn't as important to them, but they want to express their position and be respected."

Back in Kentucky, Kevin recognized that there would be an immediate reaction—as there always is—to his being named the principal at Alton Middle School. Staff members, parents, and students likely began conducting internet searches and reaching out to friends, family, and colleagues in Kevin's previous school to find out more about him. "Who is he? What's he like? What did he do at his previous school?"

These individuals began forming their impressions of Kevin—and what he would try to accomplish as a leader in their school—before they even met him. Therefore, his questions were easy for them to answer, as they likely already generated thoughts about those very questions without knowing they would be asked. It's human nature to look at someone's past and declare, "I hope they don't do that here," or "I sure hope they bring that here."

For veteran school leaders embarking on a renewal plan, these interviews may be just as eye-opening. You've been on the job for several years; you think you have a good handle on the staff and community's perceptions of the school—and you likely feel confident that you know what is going well and what needs improvement.

Be prepared—you will undoubtedly hear some responses that will make you question if the speaker is working in the same district as you. You'll hear criticisms about communication and transparency—regardless of how you've focused on those areas—and you'll likely hear praise for areas where you see the greatest need for improvement.

While you may feel your communication is a strength, there will always be those who say they aren't communicated with enough; while you can point to multiple public meetings, surveys, and presentations, there will always be those who say the budget process is not transparent enough; and while you can point to data that shows considerable student improvement in literacy scores, there will always be those who point to a higher-performing district and ask why you can't produce similar results.

The benefit you'll have as a veteran leader in your school or district is that you likely will know why certain individuals will answer as they do. However, don't let that bias discount what they are saying, for as Kevin pointed out in his core beliefs, "perception is reality."

Although your internal response may be to argue against these points, you may be better off simply accepting that these are their perceptions—their reality—and they are likely not alone. Once you accept that fact, you can begin determining how best to change their perception.

I came to realize early in my leadership career that the most oppositional members of the staff, community, or School Board force us to become better leaders. When developing proposals, reports, and presentations, I began by asking myself, "What will those highly critical individuals ask? What will they want to hear about? Where will their criticisms lie?" Rather than simply putting together my presentations assuming they would be met with support by most of the intended audience, I started developing materials with the most vocal critics in mind.

This approach made me a more effective and efficient leader. Just as a teacher cannot teach only the most accomplished students in their classroom, school leaders do not work with only the most agreeable constituents. By anticipating counterpoints and learning from the criticism directed at previous presentations, we become more adept at crafting proposals that are more readily accepted on a wider basis. While you might never achieve 100 percent success with those individuals, the effort will result in a greater level of trust with a larger audience, bringing into the fold others who might have been left outs if you only focused on those who are already strong supporters.

The second phase in Kevin's plan, *Listening, Learning, and Leading*, was scheduled to last from late summer through the first half of the school year. During this phase, individual interviews continued as the start of the academic year approached (see Table 6.2).

As staff and students returned to school, Kevin also began meeting with the School Leadership Team along with other groups such as the Parent-Teacher Organization, content area teams, and the Student Council.

Table 6.2 Phase Two: Listening, Learning, & Leading

Timeline: August
Action
1. Meet with the School Leadership Team
2. Schedule a staff meeting with all staff to review the school's Mission and Vision statements and to present the entry plan
3. Send a welcome back and introductory letter to staff members
4. Host a back-to-school assembly and hold grade-level meetings
5. Conduct beginning-of-the-year walkthroughs in every classroom and provide feedback to teachers
6. Meet with Parent-Teacher Organization
7. Meet with content-area teachers to determine expectations for collaborative planning or PLCs
Timeline: September
Action
1. Create a Principal's Advisory Council that meets monthly
Timeline: October
Action
1. Schedule visits for teachers to high-performing schools
Timeline: Ongoing
Action
1. Conduct monthly classroom walkthroughs
2. Be present during student arrivals, dismissals, and during class changes
3. Attend Student Council meetings
4. Have an open-door policy for students, parents, faculty, and staff
5. Send weekly emails to staff with updates, events, celebrations

Notably, Kevin also established a Principal's Advisory Council to meet monthly once school began, providing him with ongoing information from constituents in a smaller setting. He also made a commitment to be highly visible throughout the school—from greeting students as they arrived on campus to stopping by each classroom during the school day, modeling what we learned in Chapter 5 about the need for authentic visibility.

During the earliest days of the school year, Kevin set a high standard for communication and transparency, sending weekly updates to staff and conducting walk-through observations of each classroom, providing meaningful feedback to teachers. This effort gave teachers a clear understanding of Kevin's commitment to open communication and his focus on quality instruction as a high priority—two critical areas in which to establish high standards as you embark on your leadership journey in a new place.

If you are a veteran leader in your school or district, you likely can look back to a time when you made this level of commitment to visibility and communication. Over time, it becomes more difficult—and less of a priority—to make that same commitment. You've established relationships and routines, and as other tasks demand your time and attention, you have likely felt compelled to spend more time in your office, trusting that your staff is taking care of the kids. If this is the case, there is no time like the present to rededicate yourself to transparency and open communication. Doing so as one component in your renewal plan sends a strong message to your Board and leadership team that you are seeking continual improvement in your own practice.

A renewal plan provides the opportunity to re-engage in those activities that have been crowded out by meetings and the need to spend time in your office answering emails, writing reports, and returning phone calls. It will take intentional planning to rejuvenate your effort, but the payoff will be a more positive relationship with the school community—and more enjoyable days at work.

As a school leader, you probably did not enter the field of education envisioning days spent in your office. More likely, you pictured yourself spending your days interacting with students. However, it is likely you will find yourself in the office more than you would like to admit. I find that on those days when I can spend some time with students—whether it is standing alongside our school principals greeting students as they arrive at school, visiting classrooms to engage with students during a lesson, or serving as a guest reader in an early grades classroom—my energy and focus are better for the remainder of the day.

Kevin's intention as he began his new role in Ballard County was to maintain his focus on visibility and engagement with students and staff—a laudable goal that becomes more difficult with each passing day. By sharing this goal in writing with the staff, Kevin increased his accountability to himself and to the school—a risk he could afford to take because he was confident he would see it through.

The third phase in Kevin's plan, *Leading and Progress Monitoring*, was scheduled to last from January through the end of the academic year. Although this phase did not include formal interviews or listening sessions, it did not mean that he was done listening. His intent was that by this time, he would have interviewed all staff members, met with the Parent-Teacher Organization, visited classrooms many times, and met with the Student Council on a monthly basis, and he would have established meaningful relationships with staff, students, and parents; they would have come to trust him, and he would have led a collaborative effort to determine improvement strategies for the school.

The completion of formal interviews provided Kevin with more time to tackle the daily tasks of leading the school and begin designing and implementing improvement strategies. While he could not imagine what those strategies would be when he developed the outline of his transition plan, he knew his focus on continual improvement would require significant effort in the second half of the school year.

Prioritize Lasting *Change over* Immediate *Change*

At this point, it is appropriate to address the importance of professional restraint for educational leaders. For many new leaders—or for veterans who hear of an enticing new program or practice—the temptation to move quickly often ends in disaster. Too often, we hear of leaders who make a significant decision in isolation—or with a small group of loyal constituents who provide them with confirmation bias—without properly vetting the options with constituents who will be most impacted by the decision.

For new leaders, making radical changes before taking the time to develop trusting relationships with staff, students, and the community often results in rebellion and distrust. In those situations, as often as not, the only thing that changes for the long term is the superintendent's zip code.

In *The Trust Imperative* (2022), I shared concerns about superintendents who made decisions as significant as changing school start times during their first year on the job—without input from the community and without the benefit of having fostered trust with many constituents. In a rush to do what they felt was right, these school leaders often ended up looking for employment elsewhere, as their relationships within the community were irreparably harmed by their impatience to make a change.

If the community is not ready for change, and you, as the school leader, force it upon them, the change is not going to stick. In essence, the rush to make change results in implementation delays that can last decades as community members say things like, "Remember that superintendent who was here one year and tried to do away with our grading system?" In those cases, years and years of future students will not benefit from the new idea because the attempt to implement it came before the trust was developed.

This is not to say there won't be any decisions to make in your first year on the job. In fact, you will make dozens of decisions each day as you drink from the proverbial leadership fire hose. What you must understand is the difference between decisions that fix "broken windows," and decisions that lead to "major renovations."

Broken windows are those items that are easily addressed, require little collective effort, and result in what is generally viewed as immediate improvement. Examples of broken windows include:

- Working with your transportation director to adjust bus schedules so students no longer arrive at school before staff are on duty to supervise them.
- Working with your technology director to adopt a new platform that upgrades the district's website, web application, and rapid communications system.
- Working with your finance director to implement an online benefits enrollment system that provides employees with a better understanding of their options and an easier way to make changes.

Fixing broken windows is a trust-building activity. Notice how in each case, the change is described as "working with" others who have expertise in the area being addressed, with an effort by a small number of employees having a positive impact on a large number of constituents. These aren't decisions made in isolation that create work for others; they are decisions that have a positive impact on the culture and climate of the school.

Most broken windows are items the school has lived with for years. Just like homeowners who finally fix a shaky doorknob or a loose piece of tile once they decide to sell their home, schools often overlook minor inconveniences that could be rectified with minimal effort. When employees see these frustrating items addressed, they develop greater trust that the administration is willing to make changes that make sense.

On the other end of the change continuum are major renovations. These are changes that require a larger collective effort and will have larger, long-term impacts that may not be generally agreed upon at the outset. Major renovations include:

- Instituting a looping model at the elementary school to create opportunities for stronger relationships between teachers, students, and families.
- Flipping school start times between elementary and secondary schools to better align with research on child sleep patterns.
- Doing away with the 0–100 grading scale at the high school in order to implement standards-based grading.

While each of these major renovations is worthy of consideration, none of them should be tackled unilaterally without a great deal of faculty and community input. School leaders who take on major renovations in isolation prior to fostering trust with the staff and community will likely come up against significant pushback and risk losing any positive momentum for the school.

Leaders who take on major renovations—identifying for themselves what the problems are and what the solutions should be without significant relationship-building—often leave a trail of chaos as they move from school to school or district to district. I have heard several such individuals shrug off the controversies they have created, saying, "I'm a change agent, and change is hard for some people." I would argue that they are not agents of true change because, most often, the changes they attempt to make either do not happen at all, or are not sustained once they leave the school (which is usually soon after they have arrived).

To make lasting, impactful, positive change in your school or district, you must build trusting relationships by proving yourself as a truly collaborative leader. Major renovations in organizations—just like major renovations to large buildings—require input, expertise, and commitment from more than one person or a small group of people at the top of the organization. If you value lasting change over immediate change, you will be more likely to seek input from your staff and the school community and less likely to pull the trigger on a major renovation before those who will be doing the work understand the need and are ready to take it on. Embarking on an authentic transition plan as you accept a new position or implementing a renewal plan if you are well along in your career will help you understand where the broken windows exist and where major renovations are needed. By showing restraint and building trust first, school leaders can ensure that those new windows and renovations are impactful and durable.

For Thought and Discussion
1. Think about where you are in terms of your career in your current school or district. Would implementing a transition plan or a renewal plan make sense at this point? Why or why not?
2. Who are the people you would want to hear from if you were to begin a transition/renewal plan? What are the topics you would want to speak with them about?
3. How can leaders be *true* change agents, helping schools and communities make meaningful change, and not just creators of chaos?
4. What are some *broken windows* you'd like to fix in your school? Why haven't you taken these on, and how might you move toward addressing these needs?

5. What are the *major renovations* you want to address in your organization? How can you do this in such a way that shows you value *lasting* change over *immediate* change?

Notes

1   Estes, Kevin, Email to author, August 3, 2024.
2   Ridings, Kelley, Email to author, August 31, 2024.

7 Fostering Trust Through Professional Development

"In-service day." The mere mention of it can send some staff rushing to their doctor for a sick note, scheduling a family reunion, or devising a way to hide in their classroom without being noticed. While this sort of response is bothersome, when I look back on my own teaching career and reflect on the professional development days I experienced—and some that I led—I can see why some staff members would "head for the hills" when they have eight hours of potentially unrelatable training staring them in the face.

There are a few major challenges facing decision-makers when it comes to professional development planning for a workforce that is diverse in terms of the grade level and characteristics of the students they are teaching and the curriculum they are covering. Add to that the disparity in personal experiences, longevity, and a host of other potential differences, and it will be nearly impossible to develop one plan that meets the needs of each individual instructor.

In one classroom, you may have a veteran reading teacher with an advanced degree in literacy, more than twenty years of highly effective instruction, and a commitment to personal learning that drives them to commit many hours each year honing their skills and knowledge. This teacher is highly skilled in classroom management, and students are rarely off-task as they follow their daily routines. If you have one concern about this teacher, it is that they make use of rather traditional methods and materials and shy away from more innovative practices that may engage some of their more reluctant learners.

Next door could be a young teacher whose strengths lie in the mathematics or science fields, with a talent for using technology to boost student engagement in their lessons. Their innovative approach creates a great deal of energy in the classroom, and students indicate they love the lessons they are provided, but with fewer classroom management skills this teacher's room can often become a bit chaotic, and students often take advantage of the opportunity to be distracted and mischievous.

Just from these two brief descriptions, you are likely already formulating in your mind how you would propose assisting each of these teachers as they work to improve their craft. Hopefully, that work will center on individual feedback and personalized learning opportunities addressing their respective areas of need.

Still, there will come those moments when you, as the school leader, will be tasked with overseeing in-service planning where you must provide activities that raise the performance of all teachers. This is a truly daunting task when you think about it. Consider your own professional development experiences, especially those in which you were seated alongside colleagues from throughout your school. Are you able to identify two or three that had a significant and lasting impact on your practice? If so, reflect for a minute about why those opportunities were so meaningful for you—and if you think they were meaningful for others in your school.

It is likely that these experiences:

- addressed an area of general need or great interest
- shared meaningful data or thought-provoking ideas
- offered specific strategies for improvement
- provided ideas that were immediately implementable and sustainable

When we participate in professional learning that is viewed as a one-shot deal—such as the guest speaker who entertains us with a presentation of ideas never to be revisited—teachers can become cynical about how impactful any schoolwide learning opportunities will be for them. One needs only to scroll through the latest social media posts at the start of the school year to see how teachers feel about upcoming in-service days—and while many of those often-hilarious posts are made in jest, there is a message that should be heeded by school leaders as they plan for the days ahead. That message, most consistently, is that teachers want to spend their time in meaningful ways.

Teachers don't want to feel they have wasted time they could have used to prepare their classroom, revise pieces of their curriculum, search for new resources, or many of the other activities that improve experiences for kids that we too often expect them to do outside of the professional day. They don't want to feel mistrusted by having every minute of their day planned out with meetings and presentations. They want to be treated as professionals and as colleagues, with some input into what they need in order to step back into the classroom and provide their students with the best learning opportunities possible.

Somewhere along the line, many school leaders bought into the industrialized, assembly-line model of professional development. At worst, we treat teachers as if they are factory workers in the mid-twentieth century, punching a time clock and filling their days with rote activities meant to justify their presence at the job site. In these schools, teachers are welcomed to a professional development day by being handed an agenda that scripts out each minute—likely with a cherished ten-minute morning break and thirty minutes for lunch. Outside of those precious moments, the day is filled with meetings, presentations, and break-out sessions—right up to the final, contractually defined dismissal time.

But teachers are not factory workers, and it's no longer 1955. The profession demands a different approach. Just as innovative corporations around the world have redefined their workspaces and the workday, our teachers deserve better treatment and greater opportunities to participate in planning for their own professional development.

This requires a shift in thinking for many school leaders. For decades, we have been convinced of and comforted by the factory approach. There is great hesitancy on the part of some leaders to let go of the reins—to put away the time clock, so to speak—and to demonstrate trust in a group of individuals who are most likely quite trustworthy. Of course, there are always individuals who may look to take advantage of fewer restrictions—but part of the responsibility of being a leader is being able to manage aberrant behavior on an individual basis. We should be willing to empower the masses and address the behavior of one, providing significant benefit to the culture of the school—including students—in the long run.

Doing the Work

Conducting a Needs Assessment

One of the first mistakes we make as school leaders is to assume that we know what teachers need when it comes to their professional learning. This approach is flawed from its inception, leading to ineffective plans that miss the target—or hit the wrong target—almost without exception.

Consider, as an example, a school leader who is a strong proponent of restorative disciplinary practices in a school where such practices have not been widely practiced. This leader may decide that a workshop day dedicated to learning more about this approach may be exactly what is needed to increase staff buy-in and improve student behavior. However, staff may be feeling more of a need for information and training regarding equitable grading practices or the use of artificial intelligence in the classroom.

To avoid planning for professional learning that is not wanted, unnecessary, or repetitive, school leaders should begin with a needs assessment. By giving teachers a voice—and some choice—regarding what it is they want and need to learn about, we take the first step toward creating an empowered staff that is more likely to engage authentically in professional development activities.

One simple way to do this is by conducting an anonymous needs assessment, through which teachers respond to questions aimed at identifying the topics they want to learn about. The survey need not be lengthy or complex. A simple, seven-question, multiple-choice model is provided in Table 7.1.

Table 7.1 Teacher Professional Development Survey

Please select all options that apply.
1. What specific skills or areas of knowledge do you want to develop further to improve teaching? a) Classroom management techniques b) Integration of technology in teaching c) Differentiated instruction strategies d) Assessment and feedback methods e) Subject-specific content knowledge f) Other:_____
2. What are the most significant challenges you're facing in your teaching practice? a) Student engagement and motivation b) Time management and workload c) Addressing diverse learning needs d) Keeping up with curriculum changes e) Managing behavioral issues f) Other:_____

3. What resources or support do you need to achieve your professional development goals?
   a) Mentoring or coaching
   b) Professional development workshops
   c) Access to online learning platforms
   d) Collaborative planning time with colleagues
   e) Funding for conferences or courses
   f) Other:_____

4. Please identify any educational technologies you'd like to explore:
   a) Learning management systems (e.g., Canvas, Moodle)
   b) Interactive presentation tools (e.g., Nearpod, Pear Deck)
   c) Artificial Intelligence (AI) or Virtual reality (VR) applications
   d) Adaptive learning software
   e) Coding and robotics platforms
   f) Other:_____

5. Please identify any educational methodologies you'd like to explore:
   a) Project-based learning
   b) Flipped classroom approach
   c) Inquiry-based learning
   d) Social-emotional learning integration
   e) Culturally responsive teaching
   f) Other:_____

6. What opportunities for collaboration or peer learning would you like to pursue?
   a) Professional learning communities (PLCs)
   b) Peer observation and feedback sessions
   c) Co-teaching experiences
   d) Cross-curricular project collaboration
   e) Participation in action research groups
   f) Other:_____

7. What are your preferred learning styles or methods?
   a) Hands-on workshops and demonstrations
   b) Self-paced online courses
   c) Reading professional literature and research
   d) Attending conferences and seminars
   e) Collaborative group discussions and activities
   f) Other:_____

Clearly, these questions—and the potential responses—will change over time. Were this survey developed in 2020, it is likely that "Artificial Intelligence" would not have been an offered option. By 2024, it became the most talked about—and impactful—technological advancement of the decade. Similarly, the questions and potential responses should be adapted to meet the needs of your school, given the time and place in which you are seeking data. For example, it may not make sense to ask questions about PLCs if they are well-established in your school.

In this sample survey, offering multiple choice answers based on the current setting is helpful to spur staff members' thinking, while providing the open-ended option recognizes that they may have thoughts other than those identified in the survey.

One common mistake when conducting surveys is to try to cover every possible scenario, resulting in a lengthy survey that challenges both the respondent and those who are reviewing the responses. Shorter surveys allow respondents to answer the questions without becoming fatigued yet provide the organization with the data it needs to move forward. Depending on the topic, surveys consisting of anywhere between five and fifteen questions have proven to be the most efficient and effective in collecting the information needed.

Vetting Presenters

One of the most common criticisms of teacher professional development is that it occurs in a vacuum, highlighted by a presenter few people have heard of presenting ideas and suggestions that may never be discussed again. We've all attended presentations like this—where the speaker may be highly engaging, entertaining, and informative, but we leave the room wondering, "What's next?" Worse are those times when the presenter *isn't* engaging, entertaining, or informative, and we leave the room wondering, "What was that?"

I recall once during my time as a high school principal when I had to apologize to the staff for the presentation they had just heard. The speaker was ill-prepared, poorly spoken, and disorganized. We had essentially wasted three hours of the staff's valuable time listening to a speaker who had not been properly vetted. Teachers were feeling bored, frustrated, and disrespected—and legitimately so. The presenter didn't meet the lowest expectations we would have for one of our teachers; how could we expect staff to view them as providing meaningful information?

Recently, as I was traveling to speak at a district-wide professional development for a local school district, I received a text from my sister, a veteran teacher who was preparing for a similar day in her own district. Knowing I was about to present a workshop to a roomful of teachers, she sarcastically shared, "The only people who get excited about these PD days are the presenters, who think they have something to teach us!"

That wasn't the motivation I was looking for as I connected my laptop to the projector and watched dozens of teachers enter the conference space—many of whom, likely, were approaching the day with the same level of cynicism. Hopefully, they left the day feeling better about the experience and having some concrete ideas for improving their school, but the message my sister sent—while an attempt at humor—was instructive for me as a school leader. Teachers don't want to be entertained, dazzled, or bored during professional development times; they want meaningful programming that helps them improve their craft.

Of course, there are many examples of professional development activities that have a lasting impact, shaping instruction or promoting healthy school culture in meaningful ways—often to the point that the ideas become so ingrained that nobody remembers where they came from. When this happens, it is likely because school leadership has ensured that the learning has several characteristics:

1. The topic being covered is widely accepted or stated to be of importance to many in the school.
2. The presenter/consultant leading the work is knowledgeable, articulate, and engaging.
3. The information provided is timely, accurate, and reliable.
4. Participants are provided meaningful opportunities to engage in the work throughout the day.
5. Takeaways include specific, implementable ideas that can be adopted in individual, small group, or whole staff settings.

When all five of these qualities are in place, we have a shot at using professional development to improve student learning. Take any one of these out of the mix, and the opportunity is lost:

> Without Characteristic #1, the work is not important enough to the staff to be useful.
> Without Characteristic #2, the presentation lacks expertise and creates doubt.
> Without Characteristic #3, the information is outdated and not helpful.

> Without Characteristic #4, participants are not likely to engage for long stretches of time.
> Without Characteristic #5, participants leave without concrete steps for implementation.

Conducting the needs assessment prior to developing your schedule for professional development is a critical first step to ensure that Characteristic #1 is present. Whether that is done through a paper or digital survey or through focus group discussions, school leaders must gather input from the staff to determine where the most consistent needs exist. Failure to do so is a fatal flaw in professional development planning.

The remaining four characteristics are the responsibility of the presenter—but the school leader is the person accountable for ensuring those qualities exist through proper vetting of the facilitator. Personal experience, reference checks, and interpersonal communication with the presenter are recommended strategies for avoiding a disaster. In my experience, presenters want to do a good job for your organization. Letting them know what you are looking for is appreciated, and the more information you can provide them about your setting, the more helpful it is for them as they craft a presentation that is meaningful for your school.

In the rare case that you begin negotiating with a presenter who seems disinterested in personalizing their message for your organization, you should view that as a red flag. In my experience, adjusting a presentation to better connect with the audience usually requires a simple tweak and results in higher participant engagement. You want presenters who want to connect with the audience, and you are likely paying good money for their services, so it is not only your responsibility but also your right to share with them your expectations both for the presentation and for the takeaways for your staff.

As school leaders, we shoulder the blame if we allow learning to conclude at the end of the in-service day. Just as we too often allow strategic plans and mission statements to sit on a shelf and collect dust, rather than drive the decision-making in our buildings, we too frequently pat ourselves on the back for a great day of learning and then move on to the next item on our agenda without developing plans for further exploration or implementation of the ideas presented.

This responsibility cannot lie with the teachers—that would lead to disjointed and inconsistent application. Rather, it is up to the building or district leaders to encourage continued engagement, exploration, and innovation around the learning topic. If it is important enough to invest the district's money and the teachers' time and energy, then we must find ways to encourage the continuation of the work.

The Unconference

One of the most underutilized forms of professional development for teachers is the Unconference, or EdCamp, as it is also known. This model emerged in the early 2010s and relies upon the passions and expertise of the participants who attend this "non-agenda" event. The wonderful thing about the Unconference is that it shuns the approach that the only experts are from "away." The model empowers your staff by assuming that there is expertise to be shared within the organization. Another great thing about the Unconference is that it is low cost/high impact, and can be done with a minimal amount of planning.

Essentially, the agenda for an Unconference can be as simple as that provided in Table 7.2. The greatest pressure on the planners of the Unconference will be deciding the mechanism for identifying sessions and assigning them to rooms in your facility. New technologies make it possible to do this digitally, so each participant—no matter the size of your staff—will have the opportunity to suggest topics and sign up for different sessions in real time.

After the welcome and overview of the day, participants are asked to identify topics about which they would either like to (a) learn more or (b) share information. Once a comprehensive list is created, planners take a

Table 7.2 Unconference Agenda

- Welcome and explanation of the day
- Session Identification
- Attendee-lead sessions
- Break
- Attendee-lead sessions
- Lunch
- Attendee-lead sessions
- Break
- Attendee-lead sessions
- Adjournment

few minutes to divide the topics into the number of time periods provided during the day. To provide for robust consideration of all topics and ample opportunity for staff to select preferred topics, this "Session Identification" portion of the agenda may take up to an hour, which should provide you with at least three, if not four, workshop periods in a regular seven-hour day.

Once the topics have been identified and assigned a room, participants can sign up (if desired) or simply attend each of their preferred sessions. With few rules governing the unconference, it's easy to empower staff to attend sessions as they deem appropriate, so signing up may not be necessary—that's a local decision that may be driven by your own requirements for awarding continuing education credits.

Some districts have held unconferences with several pre-planned presentations listed at the start of the day. This can be done to generate excitement and spur thinking about other topics of interest. It is also a nice way to recognize specific staff who have identified expertise in an area of importance while providing ample opportunity for the development of session topics at the start of the unconference.

Another interesting approach to the unconference model is to team up with a school or district with whom you have not typically paired during professional development. In one district where this was done, teachers enthusiastically engaged with their colleagues from a neighboring district, developing lasting relationships that provided ongoing opportunities for shared learning in the ensuing years.

The empowering nature of the unconference structure (or lack thereof) builds trust by demonstrating trust. By turning your staff loose into self-identified learning sessions, you are demonstrating trust in their expertise and judgment of what is important, providing them with a professional development opportunity that will likely bring about meaningful change in far more personalized ways than can be accomplished by large group presentations from outside experts—for a fraction of the cost.

Internal University

One of the most consistent forms of professional development teachers enjoy is engaging in graduate coursework. This is also expensive and potentially disjointed, as teachers select individual courses and programs that may or may not be of benefit in their work at the school. While that approach allows for individual choice and should not be discarded, a more localized approach provides courses aligned directly with the district's strategic plan and areas of need, reduces costs, and—like the unconference—recognizes the expertise and passions of existing staff.

In this model, educators within the school or district are asked to submit proposals for graduate-level courses they would like to teach. "Graduate-level courses" refers to offerings that require the same time commitment and have the same expectations for learning as courses offered in the typical graduate program of nearby universities.

These proposals are submitted to the district leadership team for consideration, and several are selected each year. Courses that align with specific goals identified in the district's strategic plan, or those that address emerging needs are those most likely to be approved. The offerings are advertised to all staff, and teachers sign up to take the courses free of charge. The only cost to the district is a stipend for each of the course instructors.

As an example, several years ago we had a significant number of asylum-seeking students arrive in our district. Few of these students had any English language skills, increasing our Multi-Lingual Learner (MLL) population nearly four-fold. While we had not anticipated this influx of students in our strategic plan, we did have a legal and moral obligation to do our best for each new student, which led to a call for more education for our staff around MLL instruction.

By remaining flexible, we were better able to address student needs by meeting teacher requests for professional development opportunities that mattered at that moment. The internal course offerings allowed teachers and district leaders to identify an area of need and provide targeted instruction to address the concern.

One twist on this idea that may support teacher retention is to allow teachers to count any "credits" earned toward advancement on the salary scale. If your collective bargaining agreement provides different lanes for teachers as they earn graduate credits, providing this option for internal coursework serves as a motivator for teachers to remain with the school, as a move elsewhere will result in the loss of that recognition in the new district.

Conference Scholarships

While the unconference model can be a highly engaging way to encourage staff to learn from one another within your district, the opportunities presented to send staff out to regional and national conferences should not be ignored. Although the impact may be more myopic at first, conference attendance can result in more widespread school improvement practices when implemented properly.

Unfortunately, conferences are expensive and budgets are tight, limiting the likelihood that teachers can attend. One way around this is to work with an outside group that supports the schools—like a parent-teacher organization, an education foundation, or any nonprofit or private sector company that wishes to support professional development for educators.

In two of the districts we know of, the local education foundation agreed to work with district leadership to send teachers to conferences identified by the administration. The district leadership team identified specific conferences that were aligned with our mission and strategic planning, and teachers were encouraged to apply for scholarships to attend. The scholarships covered travel, meals, accommodation, and registration fees, and applicants were asked to describe how they would share their learning once they returned from the conference.

The release of the scholarship announcement created quite a buzz each year, and the application process became quite competitive. Unfortunately, not every applicant was provided with a scholarship, but over time, almost everyone who has applied has been able to attend these meaningful conferences and bring new ideas back to their school.

The requirement that scholarship recipients share their experiences with their colleagues and make a brief presentation to the sponsoring organization has been an important part of the program. Teachers return from their trips eager to present new ideas to their teams, and the donors enjoy hearing how their investment is paying off with innovative approaches to teaching and learning.

Prep Time

It is critical that teachers are provided time in their classrooms at the start of the year and at various points throughout each semester. They have a great deal to accomplish to make their rooms ready for student learning, and most teachers approach this work with great care and intentionality. When we disregard the importance of this work by filling their in-service days with meetings and professional development activities defined by the administration, we miss out on an opportunity to demonstrate and build trust.

The schedule for those teacher days at the beginning of the school year should be carefully crafted so that at least 50 percent of each day is provided for teachers to do their own work. Our expectations around instruction, curriculum, and engagement should be clear, and teachers should be given time to prepare to meet those expectations.

Scheduling every minute of in-service days indicates that we don't trust our teachers to do what needs to be done in preparation for students. Yet we see it over and over again—full-day agendas that provide very little room for individual work and professional judgment. Teachers leave these days feeling frustrated, disrespected, and mistrusted—and the school will be less prepared for students overall than it would be if we allowed teachers significant time to get things ready.

There isn't much we can give to our teachers to recognize their work. Time and time again we hear from teachers that *time* is the one thing they don't have enough of, and when we demand more of their time, rather than giving time back through thoughtful scheduling, we miss an opportunity to build trust. Finding the balance between the necessary meeting time for training and professional development and the chance for teachers to complete their necessary work is an absolute must for school leaders intent on nurturing a trusting work environment.

Professional development programs that recognize local needs, as well as local expertise, are strong contributors to fostering trust in the organization. When school leaders demonstrate respect for staff by valuing their time enough to offer only high-quality professional development (rather than time-fillers), and by inviting them to be the experts in areas of need, we earn trust in return.

If we can also offer exciting opportunities for individual advancement that will benefit the entire school, we create enthusiasm for a layered approach to professional development far beyond what is present when we ask teachers to file into the auditorium twice each year to hear the expert from away opine on a topic selected by the administration.

Your approach to professional development will go a long way toward defining how your staff responds to your leadership—and with many districts stacking PD days at the beginning of the school year, you can set the tone from the outset. Respecting their time, acknowledging their expertise, and engaging them in meaningful opportunities from the local to the national level is easier than you might think, and can be accomplished with thoughtful planning on your part.

For Thought and Discussion
1. Reflect back on the *best* and *worst* professional development experiences you have had as an educator. What were those experiences, and what made them awesome or awful?
2. How can you ensure professional development opportunities in your school are meaningful for all staff?
3. Take a look at the agendas for the in-service days at the beginning of the most recent school year. What percentage of the day—outside of the lunch break—was provided to teachers for their own classroom preparations? What percentage of the day was filled with staff meetings, team meetings, and other required activities? Does this reflect respect for their time? Were all of the required meetings necessary? How might you give more time to staff to take care of their classroom/instructional planning needs?
4. Identify financial resources that might be used to provide teachers with meaningful professional development opportunities, from in-house offerings to national conferences. Specific grants, donations, and budget lines may help meet this need.

5. What expertise exists within your own school/district that might be tapped to provide important professional development to staff? How could you structure these opportunities to meet the needs of the greatest number of staff on an ongoing basis?

8 Negotiating with Trust

In many parts of the United States, school budgets are deliberated and approved in a very public manner, with local voters making the ultimate decision about the level of funding to be provided for the schools. Having sat through or presented at dozens of budget meetings over the past few decades, I often find the predictability of it all somewhat amusing.

Without fail, someone will step to the microphone to oppose the spending plan, saying, "In this economy … " as if all the times that came before the present were the "good times." Of course, this is disingenuous, because the same statement was made last year—and the year before that, and the year before that—causing me to wonder, if every year is a down year for the economy, when are the up years?

It seems when economic growth is vigorous, unemployment rates are down, and the stock market is up, critics issue the proverbial doomsday warning about inflation. In years when economic growth is slow, interest rates are low, and the markets are sluggish, critics issue dire warnings of a recession. Either way, spending money on schools and increasing taxes is never, in the minds of many, a good idea.

A similar phenomenon occurs when you step into the room to begin negotiating a collective bargaining agreement for any or all of your employee units. Without fail, a School Board member will say, "This is a tough negotiations year, given the state of the nation's economy," while union representatives will unfailingly pin their arguments for significant raises and better health insurance on "the rising cost of living."

Meanwhile, the superintendent sits between the two, torn between both sides as an employee of the Board and the administrator of the collective bargaining agreement on the one hand, and the colleague and lead educator of the district's staff members on the other. This juxtaposition can be uncomfortable for even the most seasoned school leader. Staff look to you to carry their message forward to the community, while the School Board looks to you to manage the budget responsibly—and often it seems that the two are competing interests.

Many school leaders enter the bargaining session having sat on the other side of the table earlier in their career, either as a representative of the teachers' union or as the administrators' bargaining unit. While it is not unusual for superintendents to have experience in the collective bargaining process, no position you have experienced in the past will seem quite so precarious as the one in which you find yourself when sitting between the Board and the Teachers' Association.

If you argue too vociferously against the teachers' proposals, you risk losing the confidence of the largest group of professionals under your supervision. If you argue too clearly in the union's favor, you may find yourself losing the confidence of those to whom you directly report.

As superintendent, you cannot afford to lose either the trust of your staff or that of the Board. While negotiations are intended to take place in confidential executive sessions, your performance during collective bargaining will undoubtedly reverberate beyond the walls of the negotiating room. Recognizing this as yet another opportunity to build trust with all constituents, the skillful leader capitalizes on the collective bargaining process to demonstrate those qualities that both employees and Board members can appreciate: empathy, integrity, fairness, and—possibly most importantly—patience.

It is important to mention here that you can be at your best in negotiations only if you have worked to build a strong collaborative relationship with the staff. Many of the ideas shared in this book about building a culture of trust will come into play well before negotiations begin.

One step the superintendent can take to build a strong relationship with union leadership is to hold monthly meetings with union representatives in an effort to head off any potential problems before they arise. Using an open agenda format in which either the superintendent or union representatives may add items for discussion will allow the meetings to begin from a point of transparency. As with School Board meetings, taking the "no surprises" approach, with everyone agreeing to the agenda a day or two in advance of the meeting, allows for accurate information to be gathered and shared without placing anyone on the defensive.

Through these monthly meetings, the superintendent and the union develop a working relationship that is efficient and collegial, especially when both parties are interested in resolving concerns at the lowest level and keeping the school's mission at the center of the work. With this foundation laid, labor negotiations begin from a place of collaboration, rather than competition.

Approach this work with a balanced, open-minded perspective. By being deliberate and transparent about your role in the process, you can thread the needle of serving your employer—the Board—while honoring the hard work of your employees—the members of the bargaining unit.

Doing the Work

Be Prepared

One of the most important steps you can take in the bargaining process is to fully prepare the Board prior to the start of negotiations. To do this well, you should begin collecting data and creating a repository of information for the negotiating team members. While each Board may identify specific data points they'd like to consider, you might consider gathering the following prior to asking for other requests:

- The existing collective bargaining agreement (CBA)
- Leadership team concerns/proposals
- Information regarding any new federal or state laws/regulations
- Advice from legal counsel based on a review of the current CBA
- Collective bargaining agreements from comparison districts
- Salary and benefits data for all members of the unit collated onto one spreadsheet
- Salary and benefits data collated from similar districts collated onto one spreadsheet
- Selected state/regional/national data

With this information in hand, you can reach out to the Board negotiations team and ask if there are other data points they would like to consider. Adding any requested information to the file should provide you with a comprehensive view of how your agreement compares to others locally, regionally, and nationally.

Begin your preparation with an internal review of the current collective bargaining agreement. It is important to seek input not only from members of your leadership team, who are responsible for administering the contract at each of their schools, but also from district office personnel, such as staff in Human Resources, Payroll/benefits, and Finance. Building principals will likely be able to offer suggestions for strengthening articles related to workday schedules and professional responsibilities, while district office staff will offer thoughts regarding more quantitative items, like salaries, health insurance contributions, and sick bank allocations.

After you've collected input from your leadership team, take the opportunity to have the current agreement and any suggested changes from leadership reviewed by your school attorney. It's important for your attorney to know it is time to negotiate a successor agreement, and they will advise you as to any new laws that should be considered. They will also assist with structuring the wording of any new language you hope the Board will adopt as part of their proposal.

One practice that has proven to save a great deal of time and minimize confusion throughout the negotiation process is to have a digital version of the current agreement available for editing, article by article. As you prepare the Board's proposal for each round of the meetings, you can simply redline each article you hope to change and set the expectation that the union will do the same. This strategy forces each team to flesh out the language they are proposing rather than just tossing out ideas that are not fully formed, saving time and reducing misunderstandings. It also provides each side with the benefit of seeing on paper what is being suggested and provides you with a document to share with your attorney for input between sessions.

Comparison data is typically an important part of the bargaining process. Most districts have a well-defined set of organizations with whom they make comparisons on a wide range of data, from student achievement to per-pupil expenditures to interscholastic success. It makes sense that the union will also look to those districts for a comparison of CBA language and provisions.

This is a point at which the superintendent has an opportunity to build trust. You must act with great integrity and be transparent in providing all of the data from those districts with which you historically compare, even if the data supports a perspective other than that which the Board supports. We cannot cherry-pick data that supports our argument from districts with whom we share little commonality. If there are three districts you use for comparison purposes for budgeting or student performance, then you'll likely use those same three districts for comparison in the bargaining process; and if the data shows your agreement to be less generous in some areas, you simply need to be prepared to either defend that position or make adjustments.

This brings up the importance of the superintendent sharing comparison data not only with the Board's negotiating team but also with the union's team. This act of transparency will go a long way toward building trust during the process, as each team will have the same information and have the same facts from which to work. Placing all of the data on one spreadsheet and providing the file to the members of each team demonstrate an openness that will be appreciated as the data is accessed throughout the proceedings.

Finally, it is extremely helpful to create a spreadsheet of all salary and benefits data for the unit, which will allow you to calculate the financial impact of each side's proposals as you go through the process. This will be particularly important as you approach the final few sessions, when each side may be holding tight to a certain percentage increase in salaries, and they feel as if they are far apart. When you can change one number on the spreadsheet and calculate the total impact in each year of the proposed CBA, it provides each side with a more accurate understanding of the value of each proposal. You still may see sides attempting to hold the line out of principle, but with hard numbers in front of them, you may be able to help push the agreement over the finish line.

After you have reviewed the current agreement with your leadership team and attorney, collected comparison data, and created a file that will allow you to track both language and financial proposals, you should be ready to begin the bargaining process.

Engaging in the Process

I remember being greatly relieved during my first year as a superintendent when I was notified by my School Board chairperson that I would not be involved in the collective bargaining process. When I arrived in the district, all agreements were negotiated between the Board's attorney and the union's regional representative. I was told this approach had been adopted many years prior, as the Board wanted to honor the superintendent-teacher relationship and protect it from the travails of collective bargaining.

Having been part of contentious negotiations as an assistant superintendent in a previous district, my naivety led me to believe the use of a hired negotiator was a good approach. If nothing else, it meant fewer nights away from home, and—I thought at the time—less heartburn caused by listening to the one-sided arguments that often accompany each side's proposals.

Unfortunately, this also removed from the room the voices of individuals who had respectful interpersonal relationships with one another. No longer were the negotiations between the teachers and the Board members whose children they were teaching; they were now between attorneys who had been brought in by both sides, with no connection to the community, no sense of the culture that existed among the professional staff, and no real understanding of the context in which the schools operated.

When this is the format for your negotiations, you face a greater likelihood of conflict. Hired guns, so to speak, enter the room not in the spirit of collaboration, but from a competitive position. Their job is to get the best deal for their client—whichever side they represent—and their professional reputation, and therefore their livelihood, depends on their ability to close the deal with the most favorable terms for those who hired them.

Scott Menzel is the superintendent of the 20,000-student Scottsdale Unified School District, located just outside of Phoenix, Arizona.[1] A superintendent for more than twenty years now, Scott served a much smaller district in a Midwestern state at the beginning of his leadership career, and even at the start of his first superintendency, he recognized the important role he should play during negotiations.

"When I arrived, the Board had hired a negotiator to handle collective bargaining, and the union leadership implored me as the new superintendent to come to the table and lead the negotiations," Scott said. "I agreed to this on the condition that we would utilize a collaborative bargaining approach and if the tide shifted and we returned to traditional negotiations, I would again step away."

Notice that in Scott's case, even the teachers recognized the importance of a collaborative approach. They wanted district leadership at the table and were willing to drop the adversarial strategy in favor of one that relied more heavily on healthy relationships. Scott was wise enough to understand how his involvement could have an immediate positive impact.

"This was designed to foster trust and build a sense of being on the same team, working toward a shared outcome to advance the mission, vision, and values of the district," Scott said. "We were able to reach an agreement in that first year through the implementation of this process."

Without Scott's recognition of the potential he possessed, even as a new superintendent, he might have allowed negotiations to proceed in the district's traditional format, which could have resulted in irreparable harm to his reputation as a leader. This is not something leaders can afford at any point in their careers, especially not at the start of a new job.

In my own case, it took longer to realize the harm that was being done as the Board and the union remained far apart with no liaison to help bridge the gap. Once it became apparent to me that an agreement was not likely to happen, as negotiations became more contentious and teacher morale was declining, I recognized the opportunity that had been placed before me, and I was able to step into the fray, cool the temperature, and forge an agreement. Without the leadership of the superintendent, who has a vested interest in both sides' aspirations, situations like this could end up entering the more adversarial bargaining phases of fact-finding and arbitration.

The irony with the hired negotiator approach is that schools, as we all know, are a people-oriented business. Our greatest resource is our people, and the most important factor in student growth is the relationship they have with the teacher. In such a relationship-dependent environment, we should know better than to remove those personal connections from the equation and adopt an adversarial approach to collective bargaining.

While this is not the recommended strategy, if this is to be your approach to negotiations, you must enter the process with your eyes wide open, recognizing that you must remain in close contact with the negotiator throughout the process. They will most likely seek clarification on your desired outcomes, but you should also share with them the good things about the employees who work in the district and your desire to maintain a positive relationship with the staff. Help the negotiator understand where you are willing to compromise and where you feel the need to stand firm, so they can strategize with you how to approach each session.

Frequent communication with your Board chairperson and the hired negotiator may allow you to influence the messaging that is sent during the bargaining sessions, though it's not the same as being there. You will want to stay very close to the process and seek opportunities to interject if you sense that the tenor is becoming more contentious than productive.

The preferred format for negotiations places the superintendent in the room with teacher leaders and members of the Board. Unless there is an unlimited supply of financial support authorized by the Board (unlikely) matched by a reasonable request for adjustments to salaries and benefits by the union (also unlikely), the two sides will need someone in the room who can calm the waters when the turbulence begins. By removing the superintendent from the room, the district is left without a moderator with a vested interest in a collaborative settlement. Instead, lines are drawn, participants choose their sides, and the battles begin.

Just as important is the fact that engaging in the process allows the superintendent to hear the concerns and priorities of the teachers and to speak to the concerns of leadership. While negotiations are not a place to air grievances, they can be a productive setting for addressing concerns related to the CBA. Do teachers have a strong desire to amend the parental leave provisions in the Agreement, or is maintaining health insurance their biggest concern? Are salaries going to be the sticking point in negotiations, or are employees more interested in adjusting the language regarding compensatory time for parent-teacher conferences? Are school leaders concerned that the use of sick days near vacation periods is becoming problematic, or is it more important that they lower the budgetary impact of health insurance contributions?

While it's likely that all these items—and more—will be part of the discussion, the superintendent's presence in the room ensures there is a clear understanding of what the teachers are asking for—and what the Board is willing to provide—as negotiations unfold. Serving as the moderator, you can rephrase statements, clarify positions, and interject data that supports or refutes claims made at the table.

Most importantly, because of your desire to reach an agreement that meets the needs of both parties, it is critical for you to play an active role in the process. By setting up the schedule, organizing the agenda, openly sharing data, and helping to craft, compare, and track proposals, both the Board and the employees experience your leadership in a tangible way. Making the commitment to engage in the process is the first step; once you are on board with this approach you can deliberately and thoughtfully take on the tasks that make the process a productive one for everyone involved.

Schedule with Intention

The first negotiating challenge will be to develop a schedule that works for all participants in the bargaining process. It is helpful to generate a list of potential dates on which all members of the Board's negotiating team are available first and then confirm which dates work for the employees' negotiating team. The goal is typically to find six to eight dates for which all team members are available, exuding a sense of optimism that the process can be completed within that timeframe.

Once you have potential dates agreed upon, it is important to publish the schedule for all participants. Rather than having an open-ended schedule, identify the proposed endpoint of the process, including the dates by which the union and the Board will approve the agreement. A sample schedule is provided in Table 8.1.

Set Clear Expectations and Protocols

As noted in Table 8.1, the first meeting agenda includes time to agree upon the norms by which all team members will abide. This is yet another step that builds trust, as both sides agree on clearly stated protocols governing both the overall process and the behavior during meetings.

Table 8.1 Negotiations Timeline

Prior to October 1	Union and Board meet separately to identify interests
October 1	Initial Meeting • Introductions • Confirm Schedule • Agree on norms and protocols • Share interests • Union Proposal #1
October 15	Meeting #2 • Board Response to Proposal #1
November 1	Meeting #3
November 15	Meeting #4
December 1	Meeting #5
December 15	Meeting #6
January 1	Union ratification
January 15	School Board approval

Table 8.2 Negotiations Protocols

1. The participating bodies are the School Board (SB) and Educators' Association (EA).
2. Any observers of the process will be by mutual consent of the SB and EA. Observers will not participate in the process.
3. Resource persons may participate fully during the process and may caucus with their designated body.
4. Caucusing is allowed at any time, upon request by either party.
5. Each participating body shall, in a timely manner, supply the other with requested information in its possession that is not legally protected from disclosure.
6. Tentative agreements (TAs) may be reached at any time. TAs are conditional and may be subject to agreement on other items (e.g. TAs relative to language may be contingent upon agreement on salary and benefits).
7. No electronic recording is to be made of any of the proceedings without the mutual consent of both parties.
8. Meetings will be conducted in Executive Session. The public will not have access to these proceedings.
9. After the third negotiating session (Meeting #3) there will be no new proposals submitted by either the SB or the EA without mutual consent by both parties.

A sample of negotiating protocols is provided in Table 8.2, followed by a short list of meeting norms in Table 8.3. It is worthwhile to spend several minutes near the beginning of the first meeting going through the protocols and norms, setting the tone for professional, efficient meetings where respect for others is paramount.

Ensure that each participant in the bargaining process understands and agrees to the protocols and meeting norms, going so far as to have the team leader for each side sign off on the protocols as the first item of agreement. This also provides written confirmation of the agreement should you need to refer to it later in the process.

It is helpful to identify the resource persons referred to in item #3 of the protocols. For the Board, this is typically the superintendent and may also include other central office personnel, such as the director of finance, HR, or payroll. The union may identify representatives from their statewide association or previous members of their negotiating team. Of course, either side may list their legal counsel. Regardless of who is identified, each side should attempt to name those individuals at the start of the process and avoid surprising their counterparts on the other side of the table.

Table 8.3 Meeting Norms

1. We will begin and end on time.
2. Only one person will speak at a time.
3. This is a bargaining session, not a grievance hearing.
4. This is a confidential session; conversations will remain in the room.
5. All participants agree to limit use of electronic devices, including texting, to emergencies, and will leave the room if it is necessary to use their phone/laptop/tablet, etc.
6. We will respect others' needs, including the option to pass if asked a question.
7. Each of us agrees to share the air and be concise in our communication.
8. Both sides will come prepared to each meeting with factual information.

The phrase—"the other side of the table"—brings up an interesting point. The physical arrangement of the room in which negotiations take place matters. Collective bargaining can be adversarial by its very nature, and to be at our best throughout the process, we should attempt to remove those structures that create a sense of *us versus them*. When teams enter the room and sit on opposite sides of the table from one another, the physical barrier of the table and the huddled nature of the seating do nothing to diminish the potential sense of conflict.

A better approach is to organize the seating in a circle or square, with members from each team dispersed throughout the room in a less rigid format. This creates a greater sense of collaboration and sends the message that we are not on opposite sides; we are all working toward the same mission, though we may have competing ideas on how to get there.

Ask team members to be deliberate about not sitting next to one of their own teammates when they enter the room—which also leads to polite conversation between and among teams as everyone gets settled. In fact, you may find that it is difficult to get the entire group to turn their focus to negotiations as they become more comfortable with one another and enjoy catching up on recent events in the schools.

Along with arranging the room and seating so it is conducive to collaboration, you should take steps to make sure everyone is comfortable throughout the meeting. By providing snacks and water and letting everyone know where they may find items like the coffee maker and restrooms, you set a tone of respect and professionalism that invites collaboration.

Finally, it is important to have a secondary space near the negotiation room, providing for one of the teams when the time comes for confidential discussions, or what many refer to as a caucus. Either side should be able to request a caucus at any point in any meeting to firm up their response to a specific item. It is helpful to indicate how long the caucus will be so that neither side is left sitting for lengthy periods of time.

Preparing the space for collaborative discussions and agreeing upon the schedule and protocols at the start of the process send a strong message to all participants that negotiations should be respectful and collegial to the greatest extent possible. With this foundation in place, you are less likely to be faced with a breakdown in communication later—and if you are, you have a good place to which you can reset if necessary.

Begin with Interests

Much has been written about interest-based bargaining, and school leaders should do their own research to identify strategies that may be beneficial to their specific setting. In most school districts with a clear mission statement and collaboratively developed strategic plan in place, the interests of the district are easily identified—and it is hoped that the interests of the union are aligned.

However, in many situations, the interests of the union—at least as far as they pertain to collective bargaining—may be more slanted toward employee rights and benefits than student growth and development. This is why negotiating becomes challenging for everyone involved; the Board wants to hire and retain the best educators for their students while protecting against significant tax increases, and the union wants to provide the best educators for the district while elevating employee protection and compensation.

Regardless of whether you elect to employ traditional or interest-based bargaining, it is good practice to have each negotiating team share their core interests at the start of the process. In doing so, each team is provided with a clear understanding of what is important to the other, and they can begin to formulate ideas about how to address those interests.

The union may indicate that they are concerned about teacher retention—especially if there has been a recent exodus of staff to nearby districts. They may also be concerned about teacher stress levels, leading to health issues. In a related interest, the Board may state concerns about employee attendance and its impact on student learning. With each team's main interests on the table, you can begin to share proposals for addressing those concerns, starting with the initial proposal from the union.

Track Progress

One critical role for the superintendent during negotiations is to deliberately facilitate the sessions. Aside from developing the timeline for the process, agendas for each meeting, and a welcoming physical environment, this includes ensuring the group's collective progress is not lost and there is no confusion regarding what has been proposed and agreed upon.

As was mentioned earlier, by agreeing that each proposal will be presented as a red-lined version of the articles being amended, each team is taking a step toward simplifying the tracking of progress. By sharing these proposals electronically, the superintendent can make edits to each proposal as bargaining ensues, adding signature lines for articles on which a tentative agreement is reached.

It is important for everyone in the room to understand why these are called *tentative* agreements. It is helpful to explain that agreements are not finalized until the full membership of the union and the full School Board has voted to approve. By signing tentative agreements, each side is indicating their willingness to present the proposed language to their respective membership. The tentative agreements allow each team to move to the next item, feeling positive about progress being made and compromises offered by each side.

As you sign tentative agreements, you begin to reduce the number of items on the table, eventually getting to the point where each participant can see the light at the end of the tunnel. This can have an encouraging effect on the process, as each team checks off agreement on various articles.

Tracking progress in this manner also ensures arguments about tentative agreements are not part of future agendas. The lead negotiator for each side signs off on the TA after carefully reading the language, removing the claim "we didn't agree to that" which may occur if tracking is not done effectively. Nothing derails negotiations more quickly than one team feeling the other has taken liberties with statements that were made during the process and exaggerated their counterpart's agreement on one or more proposals.

Close the Deal

There is no question that a settled collective bargaining agreement is a benefit for the superintendent. Employees "working without a contract" feel disrespected, unheard, and devalued. This sort of culture is unhealthy for staff and has a detrimental impact on students. The lack of a settled agreement often leads to "work to rule" practices and other strategies that are designed to let the School Board know how far beyond the CBA's provisions teachers are willing to go on a regular basis. Such practices, employed as emotional responses to a conflict between the Board and the union, hurt students.

When educators go against their natural tendencies and refuse to help students outside of their contracted work hours, it has a lasting impact on the school's culture. A safe supportive, engaging culture may be the most important characteristic of a high-performing school, and few leaders enjoy a lengthy, impactful career when the culture of their school is one of conflict and mistrust.

A settled agreement is of primary importance to the superintendent. Understanding the critical nature of bringing both teams together to forge that agreement is not something any superintendent should take lightly. Aside from making sure the information presented in each proposal is factual and accurate, the superintendent may also act as a liaison between the two sides, carrying messages back and forth during caucuses and helping each side to see the value in the other's proposals.

While it is important to remember that it is the Board to whom you ultimately report, it is also worth noting that it is the employees with whom you work each day and who you rely upon to carry forth the district's mission and core values through their work with students. Carefully ensuring that each side hears the message from the other—and stepping in to ensure those messages are delivered accurately and respectfully—the superintendent can help ensure the bargaining process is completed efficiently and with a minimum of conflict.

For Thought and Discussion

1. As you look ahead to the next round of labor negotiations, what can you do to build a relationship with union leadership? Are there communications they would appreciate from you, or opportunities for engagement in decision-making? How might you reach out to them to forge a relationship that will make negotiations more collegial for all involved?

2. What negotiation practices have been in place in your district that impede progress toward a settled CBA that everyone can live with? Are the right people in the room? Have relationships been formed that might be leveraged more effectively in the process? Is meaningful data readily available and shared with both teams?

3. What concerns does the union have with the current CBA that you might be able to support in your confidential conversations with the Board? Are there items you can identify that may provide opportunities for compromise?

4. Take some time now, before negotiations begin, to set up payroll and benefit spreadsheets that can be adjusted easily each year. Work with your data or HR team to create the files so a simple change to a percentage point will recalculate salaries and benefits for every employee in the unit and allow the Board and union to understand the financial impact of each proposal.

5. How important is it for your district to be operating with settled bargaining agreements? Consider the cultural impact of protracted labor disputes. Where does that balance lie between maintaining employee morale and recognizing taxpayer capacity to pay? This is a conversation you should define for yourself before entering the negotiating room.

Note

1 Menzel, Scott, Email to author, July 23, 2024.

9 **Building Student Trust**

Through three decades of work as a school leader and nearly a decade of teaching graduate courses to aspiring school leaders, I have to admit that much of the focus of our discussions around leadership has had to do with the leadership of staff. This is not surprising; effective school leaders spend a great deal of time and energy determining how best to engage staff when identifying challenges, determining potential solutions, and designing and implementing those solutions. Collaborative leadership requires great intentionality and consistency, both of which require significant attention from the person in charge.

While there is no doubt that superintendents, principals, and other school leaders will spend much of their time interacting with adults (teachers, coaches, advisors, etc.), there will also be important student-centered work to be done by school leaders to ensure learning takes place in a high-trust environment. While all students enjoy enhanced engagement in a trusted culture, the benefits are particularly noticeable for students in certain grades and those coming from a home environment that lacks trust. Experienced educators are aware—and new educators will soon learn—that for some students, the school can provide the safest, most stable environment they will encounter.

We cannot assume that all students will enter the building sensing the care and empathy we have for them. In fact, some will enter the school with a healthy distrust of adults—which means we must be deliberate in the actions we take to demonstrate concern for their well-being. When educators take for granted student trust, we overlook opportunities to be intentional about ensuring and deepening that trust.

It is sometimes said that in every interaction we have with another human being, we either build trust or degrade trust. While we may not think of our interactions with another person in that specific manner, it is worth considering that as school leaders, our day-to-day interactions and actions have an impact on the level of trust with which we—and, by extension, the schools—are viewed.

In his book *Grading with Equity*, Joe Feldman reminds us that the greatest point at which a student will decide whether an adult can be trusted is the moment when they make an error.[1] This is one profound statement in a book filled with data-supported ideas that enhance trust in the school through thoughtful grading practices. Expanding Feldman's theory to the entire school, we are challenged to be more intentional about addressing student errors—both those that are academic and require "grading" and those that are behavioral and require intervention, restoration, and/or discipline.

Throughout this chapter, we will explore actions school leaders have taken to nurture student trust. The practices shared here should be scalable to any school or district, regardless of size, though—as always—school leaders seeking to integrate any new strategy should carefully consider the nuances of their own setting and work collaboratively with individuals who can assist with the development of the local program.

Doing the Work

Providing Safe Schools

As was discussed earlier, research indicates that adult workers perform more effectively in a high-trust setting, and it is not a stretch to assume that students are no different; any research studying the impact of high- and low-trust environments on adults will produce results that hold true for our students. Fear, anxiety, intimidation, confusion . . . all of these interfere with the brain's ability to perform at its highest level, resulting in a negative impact on performance.

Consider a sixth-grade student entering a classroom corridor at their middle school at the beginning of the school day. The corridor is filled with adolescent energy; dozens, if not hundreds, of students are loudly interacting with one another, jostling one another with their oversized backpacks, and both verbal and physical contact with others is virtually impossible to avoid. There is no teacher in sight—they are in their classrooms busily preparing for the first lesson of the day, which is just moments away.

All this student can see is a corridor full of loud, energetic students—most of whom are larger than they. It is an intimidating space and a scary way to begin the day—and even though the adults are convinced the student is safe, we must recognize that for the student, the setting may not *feel* safe.

Now imagine that same student entering the same corridor, with the same number of fellow students present—but in this case, there is a teacher standing outside each classroom, interacting with students as they pass by. As the student looks down the corridor, they can see teachers smiling at students, asking them about last night's concert or game, and offering words of encouragement about the day ahead.

Suddenly, this once-intimidating space feels much safer. The student is confident they will be unimpeded on their trip down the corridor; their trust in the school is deepened, and they can focus on academics, rather than nervously navigating the gauntlet known as the middle school hallway.

From this simple example, experienced educators can likely see the impact on students when they feel safe and can trust that the school will keep them safe. Only then can they put forth their best and most focused effort academically.

We begin with the need to develop trust by ensuring that students *are* safe and *feel* safe throughout their school experience. We must separate these two things from one another because they are truly independent phenomena. This is not something all school leaders understand, which I can attest to because of my own shortsightedness in this area during the early stages (at least) of my leadership career.

As a high school principal, I could readily declare that our school was, for the vast majority of students a vast majority of the time, a safe place. Our discipline data supported this statement, as we had very few reported incidents of physical altercations, harassment, or bullying each year. Students were "where they were supposed to be when they were supposed to be there" treating one another and their teachers with respect, and each school day was marked by order and a sense of calm.

Through consistent effort, the teachers and administrators at the school were able to create an environment in which we could point to the data and say, "Students *are* safe in our school." And yet, our school counselors, nurses, and administrators were inundated each day with students who did not *feel* safe, finally leading to the understanding that being safe and feeling safe are, indeed, two different things. Much like the toddler who is afraid of the monster under their bed, students have many reasons for feeling unsafe, and while the threat may not seem real to us the impact on learning when one feels unsafe certainly is.

To promote a culture in which students *feel* safe, we must develop and implement systems, routines, and protocols to ensure they *are* safe, acknowledge those times when they feel unsafe, and make every effort to address the things we cannot see. Only after achieving actual safety can we effectively address students' feelings of safety.

We've already identified the importance of adults being visibly present and engaging with students in informal settings throughout the school. By clarifying the importance of this effort for your staff, you will likely get the buy-in necessary to make it happen, though it will undoubtedly take frequent reminders throughout the year to maintain the effort. The following examples describe a variety of additional actions school leaders have taken to address student safety and, therefore, student trust.

Creating a Welcoming Environment

Imagine you are the parent of a student arriving at your school—regardless of grade. On this day you are driving your child to school, as it fits into your schedule to do so. As you pull up to the school, many other students are arriving at the same time. Dozens, if not hundreds, of students are clamoring off school buses, out of vehicles, or arriving by bicycles or walking paths. Other than parents dropping off their children at the curb, no other adults are in sight as students disappear into the building. You notice a few students jostling one another—and maybe even two or three students apparently laughing or making fun of another student.

As your child prepares to step out of your vehicle and enter this sea of energy, you have that momentary sense of angst, hoping they are not one to be picked on—nor one to join in and pick on others. You want to protect them and guide them at the same time—but your day beckons, you realize your child must learn to navigate society on their own, and you trust that adults inside the school will be present to keep things orderly once the students enter the building.

Now shift to a different day. On this day as you drop your child for the day, the school principal is standing outside the entrance to the school. They warmly greet students by name as they arrive, holding the door and commenting positively on things like last night's game, the school play, or a brightly colored backpack—things that matter to the students. You notice none of the students jostling one another or taking intimidating stances toward one another, and your child enters the school feeling welcomed and embraced.

What a difference in these two scenarios—and such a simple, yet often challenging, strategy to employ. By being present and visible at the start of the school day—as students arrive outside the building—school leaders send a strong signal to the students, parents, and anyone else watching that student safety and engagement are a priority at their school.

Clearly, many things can get in the way of this practice. Early morning meetings, unexpected phone calls, hallway conversations with staff members, or a spilled cup of coffee in the lobby—just about anything can call a school leader away from this daily task. Principals should enlist the help of assistant principals, athletic directors, deans of students—even superintendents—to be part of the greeting crew so that others are there to fill the gap when needed.

Students are not the only ones to benefit from this engaging start to the day. When school leaders and their staff members begin the day interacting informally and pleasantly with students, their own outlook brightens. They enjoy a bit of laughter, they see their students in a different light, and they begin to know their school even better as they start to notice patterns in student attendance, behavior, and relationships that impact their day at school.

Ensuring Students Are Known

One of the most important ways to develop student trust in the school is to promote meaningful relationships between students and staff members. Educators often hear it said that each student needs at least one adult in the school with whom they seek counsel, confidence, and trust. This should not be left to chance. While schools are typically filled with educators who understand the importance of positive relationships, intentional schoolwide efforts that promote meaningful interactions with students must be a foundational commitment of each school.

Dr. Ken Nye was a longtime high school principal, author, and graduate instructor, and one who left a mark on the schools he led that remains today, more than twenty-five years after he last served as principal. While at Yarmouth High School, just outside of Portland, Maine, in the 1980s and 1990s, Ken led the school to adopt innovative programming which has remained in place through more than three decades and at least six successive principals.

Most notably, Ken's school of 550 students was an early adopter of the need for meaningful relationship-building between adults and students. As a result, in the 1990s the school instituted a thoughtfully crafted, collaboratively developed student advisory program in which every professional educator was assigned eight to ten students with whom they met every day for the entirety of the student's four years of high school.

The structures of such a program may be found in many high schools, but—as was mentioned in Chapter 2—oftentimes structures are not used as intended. In the case of advisory programs, they often become just another "homeroom" with very little interaction between students and teachers. This was not the case in Yarmouth, where Ken and his team implemented the program in a collaborative manner that has led to remarkable importance and sustainability.

First and foremost, the entire staff bought into the program and its purpose. Chalk this up to Ken's collaborative approach in which staff were engaged in identifying the need for stronger relationships between students and staff. Secondly, the advisory period was prioritized in the daily schedule, and teachers were provided training prior to implementation, along with grade-specific activities to conduct with students throughout the year. Finally—and possibly most powerfully—the administration modeled the importance of the program by serving as advisors themselves.

The advisory program continues to be a hallmark of the school's culture to this day. Throughout their four years at the school, students meet daily in advisory to discuss matters of importance to the school (e.g., concerns around bullying, fan behavior at games, artificial intelligence in the classroom) while also addressing student-based needs such as academic support, course sign-ups, standardized testing, and the like.

At the end of four years of high school for each student, there are several very visible signs of the impact of the advisory program—for both students and faculty. One occurs at graduation, where students receive their diplomas directly from their advisor rather than from the superintendent or a Board member. As the principal reads each graduate's name, the student's advisor steps out from the group of senior advisors to hand the diploma to the student. What is observed by the audience is a moment of unbridled joy as students walk—or run or skip—across the stage into the arms of their advisors. No obligatory handshake is necessary—the hugs are enthusiastic and authentic, as are the tears that often flow from the advisors and students as they say "goodbye" after four years of daily contact.

Another indicator of the buy-in and impact of this program is demonstrated by veteran teachers, who often schedule their retirement date to coincide with the graduation of their senior advisees. Rather than retiring at their earliest eligibility, staff will frequently choose to remain at the school until their current group of advisees graduate. On the rare occasion when an advisor leaves the school prior to their advisees graduating, they are invited back for the commencement ceremony, where they stand alongside the new advisor, handing out diplomas and hugs as the graduates cross the stage.

It is not just the high school and middle school where students benefit from feeling seen and known. At the elementary level, students are quite new at forming relationships with adults outside of their family unit. It is critical for the school to provide relationships that nurture each child's individuality while respecting the norms of the group. Holding a "morning meeting" at the start of each day is the elementary model of the advisory program—an opportunity for students to share items of importance to them and get to know one another and their teacher in a setting that is not purely academic, ultimately creating an environment that allows for feelings of comfort and safety that enhance learning for each child.

Honoring Student Voice

A significant characteristic of a trustworthy person is empathy—the ability to place oneself in another's shoes and understand what it is they are feeling or experiencing. For many years (decades or centuries, even) student voice was not something that was given much consideration in K-12 schools. Sure—most high schools had a student council that claimed to be a form of "student government," but they were largely tasked with planning Spirit Week each year and maybe proposing better pizza in the school cafeteria. Beyond that, decisions were made at the highest levels of the organizational chart with little or no input from students.

In recent decades, high schools in particular—and middle schools on a growing basis—have sought student voice on a wide range of topics from the daily schedule to student handbooks. Students are provided with seats on the local School Board, participate on interview committees for new teachers, and serve in a variety of capacities to lend their perspective to school improvement efforts. Elementary school leaders are also recognizing the power of student voice, asking students to serve on playground design committees and civil rights teams at the earliest grades in their respective schools.

How, why, and when leaders provide students with an opportunity to share their ideas vary from school to school, but the final result is that students feel a greater level of trust in the school and feel more vested in—and accountable to—the decisions made. There are a lot of great examples of this work if we're willing to look for them, and each can be easily modified to fit the setting in our own district.

Interview Teams and Sample Classrooms

At some point in each of the graduate courses I teach, I pose the question, "What is the single most important thing school leaders should do to foster student trust in the school?" The answers are many and varied. Some participants offer well-meaning but not-too-specific ideas such as "Give students a voice" or "Listen to the kids." Others suggest more targeted strategies like "provide open campus" or "implement restorative justice."

There isn't a thought that has been shared in these sessions that has sounded like a bad idea—and many of these suggestions are discussed elsewhere in this book. However, there is one answer that resonates most loudly, and that is ensuring that we hire highly qualified professionals who care about students, like working with students, and can engage with and relate to students in meaningful ways. If we do that successfully in every hire we make, our jobs as school leaders become much easier and student lives become more fulfilling.

Imagine the life of a school leader in a building or a district where every employee is a high performer, including:

- Bus drivers who know each of their students—not just by name and address, but by their parents, their siblings, and their interests. They

greet their riders warmly every morning, ensure their safety and comfort throughout the trip to and from school, and send them off for the afternoon with a sincere wish for a great evening.
- School nutrition workers who enjoy knowing and serving students and recognize the importance of savory, nutritious food served in a comfortable, welcoming environment.
- Custodial and maintenance staff who take pride in a clean, functional facility and see their position as one of important service to the students, staff, and community—and who understand their role in promoting the school's mission and core values.
- Educators—including paraprofessionals, specialists, counselors, teachers, and administrators—who are driven to ensure the students are well-cared for, given expert instruction, and provided with innovative opportunities with meaningful feedback.

In a school filled with caring, expert professionals with integrity, student and family trust in the organization is high—and the job of the school leader becomes more manageable—and more enjoyable. Experienced administrators know all too well the time and energy it takes to address poor performance by any singular employee. Even an isolated complaint about a staff member can take days to address and resolve, making the hiring of high-functioning employees a critical part of any leader's organizational improvement plan.

There are several barriers for school leaders to overcome to hire the best staff effectively. Most notably, staff shortages in all job categories are making it difficult for school leaders to commit to rigorous hiring practices, leading to the "warm body" approach to hiring in which schools believe—and practice—that *anybody* being hired to a position is better than *nobody*, likely resulting in perfunctory hiring practices that produce mediocre results.

Another barrier to filling schools with high-performing staff is what can be referred to as the "resolved mediocrity" approach. Too often, school leaders allow themselves to subscribe to the belief that "the staff is who the staff is" and there will be few opportunities to make improvements through the hiring process.

While it is true that continuing contracts, tenure, and collective bargaining agreements encourage less turnover in schools than might be seen in other sectors of the economy, a realistic look at the number of new staff hired at schools each year would likely reveal that, within a few short years, school leaders can make enough new or replacement hires to noticeably impact the culture within the school. With more and more educators opting to change professions earlier, the opportunity to institute rigorous hiring practices and draw the highest quality candidates will increase.

Too often, though, we rely on the traditional format of hiring. You know the drill: Ask each applicant to submit their credentials and write an essay, conduct two very similar rounds of interviews with a committee of willing employees, conduct a final interview with the principal or superintendent, check references, and make the hire.

A preferred process invites input from students, regardless of their grade level. One way to do this is to include students on the interview team. While this is a step in the right direction, the input you receive will still be limited to the opinions of one or two students who were likely chosen because of their adult-like qualities. A more engaging approach is to have one interview team composed of adults and a second team composed entirely of students, with the two teams meeting after each round of interviews to discuss their reactions to each candidate. In this model, students are also engaged in developing the questions they will ask of each candidate, and a student leader facilitates the interview itself.

Aside from having more students involved in the process, one benefit of this approach is that the students see how the candidate interacts with students with whom they may be working—without other adults in the room to influence the climate. There may be a stark difference between a candidate's ability to answer questions asked by other adults sitting in a conference room and their prowess in interacting with students in a less formal setting.

Another strategy for increasing student input is to require candidates to teach a sample lesson in a setting similar to that for which they are applying, giving an entire classroom of students the opportunity to share their thoughts about the applicant. While teaching the sample lesson, the candidate is observed by several members of the interview team, including a member of the administration. Observers make notes using the district's observation tool, and students are provided with a survey at the end of the lesson, regardless of the grade level being taught. Providing students with anonymous methods of sharing their thoughts allows you to develop a more candid analysis of each candidate's performance.

Not surprisingly, from the inception of this practice in one district in which I worked, we began to see shifts in the order of preference that had been determined after the initial interviews. Our experience has been that candidates who were at the top of our list after the interview remain there only about 60 percent of the time after the model lesson.

This means in a school in which ten new teachers are hired each year under the "two-interview" model, leaders may be hiring four instructors who may not have been the strongest candidates within the applicant pool—which means dozens of students may not be receiving the best instruction possible had the school employed a more rigorous hiring practice.

Note, as well, the engagement of students in the hiring process. Even at the youngest levels, candidates are observed interacting with potential students, and students are provided the opportunity to share their feedback on the candidate's performance. At the high school, the interview with the student panel provides students with an opportunity to develop their own feel for each candidate and to share their thoughts directly with the staff interview team. At all levels, the sample lesson tells us far more about the applicant's ability to relate to students than any interview responses will provide.

Through these two settings—the student interview panel and the model classroom lesson—students are empowered to have a say in the professionals who will be serving them. While this is a trust-building activity in and of itself, the hiring of candidates who have demonstrated the greatest capability to relate to students has an even longer impact on the culture of the school.

Students who participate in the process often take some ownership in the individuals being hired, as we hear students greet new teachers by proudly declaring, "I was on your hiring team!" This feels like a "we're in this together, and I want you to succeed" moment that would not be possible under the traditional two-interview format.

When hiring administrators, the second round becomes trickier, but with some creativity, schools can design hiring processes that bring out the best qualities of the leading candidates. Examples of impactful second-round activities include:

- When hiring a school principal, ask candidates to facilitate a thirty-minute meeting in which they collaborate with learning area leaders to determine the professional development schedule for the first

teacher day(s) of the school year. It's not important that they leave the mock meeting with a fully developed plan; what you are looking for is the candidate's ability to develop an agenda, communicate the goals of the meeting, listen intently to others' ideas, and wrap up the meeting with clear next steps to be taken.
- When hiring a district-level director (e.g., Curriculum or Special Education), have each candidate facilitate a meeting with key personnel to address an item of concern in the district. It may be meeting with grade-level leaders to design the beginning steps toward review of a reading or mathematics program at the elementary school, or meeting with special education leaders to develop a training schedule that provides paraprofessionals with the skills and certifications required of them in self-contained classrooms.

In each setting, a "fishbowl" arrangement, with participants sitting with the candidate in the center of the room and observers seated around the perimeter, allows for meaningful observations by each member of the team. Following the activity, ask the candidate to assess their own performance.

- What went well?
- What would they like to have done differently?
- Where would they see things going from here, had this been a real meeting?

Once the candidate leaves the room, it is important to gather thoughts from those who participated in the mock meeting. Ask them to respond to prompts such as:

- How well did they feel the candidate listened to them?
- Did they feel the meeting flowed in a logical and efficient manner?
- What about the candidate's leadership style made each participant comfortable/engaged/uncomfortable?

These insights are critical, especially in a well-designed activity in which the participants are staff members who will be working with the new leader and where the topic is one of importance to the school.

Regardless of the methods you use for hiring, including student voice and placing candidates in settings similar to those they will experience in the workplace are critical to hiring the best educators for your students, which may be the biggest trust-building endeavor you will undertake as a school leader.

Allowing for Informal Input

My son, Caleb, was a fairly energetic fourth-grader whose favorite subject in school was—like that of many youngsters—physical education. In fact, the only part of his day about which he was more passionate than physical education was recess.

At some point during the school year, it appears Caleb and his friends became a little too competitive during the recess soccer games, and the teachers decided it would be in the best interest of all to take a break from competitive play at recess. The soccer balls and basketballs were removed from the playground, and a moratorium was placed on competitions of any kind.

This decision stirred up the social activism that had previously lain dormant in my ten-year-old son. He arrived home from school and announced that he was starting a petition and he was going to get his friends to picket the school and "boycott" recess.

As the high school principal in a neighboring community, I was sympathetic to the position my elementary school colleague would be in should the petition and picketing take place. While it was likely to be an innocuous event, it also appeared to be a more "aggressive" response than might be necessary for the students to have sports reinstated at recess.

With that in mind, I encouraged my son to consider a more personal approach. "Maybe you could write your principal a letter and ask to meet with him and present your ideas," I offered. "That would give him an opportunity to hear your perspective, and you might find him willing to consider a change without all the effort of a petition and sign-making."

Caleb went to work on the family computer and composed a letter to his principal, Mr. Porter. The following day, he delivered the following note to the school's office:

> *Dear Mr. Porter-*
> *I, along with others, am unhappy about the duty teachers taking away all the sports at our recess. I have asked people at other recesses and they have said that they still have sports. I hope that by working together we can get most of the sports back at recess so that my friends and I don't have to just walk*

around. I would like to help so that my friends and I can enjoy recess again. Please let me know what I can do. Thank you for listening to me.
Caleb Dolloff, Room 1

To his credit, Mr. Porter seized this opportunity to work directly with the students to develop a plan that would provide students with free-play activities they enjoyed, while re-emphasizing the school's core values.[2] He met with Caleb and a few of his friends, and they developed a plan that allowed for the reinstatement of sports at recess with clearly defined expectations for behavior.

It is quite likely that Mr. Porter had some work to do to convince the teachers on recess duty that this was a good idea. Kudos to him for placing a priority on student voice while also setting the expectation that the school's core values would be upheld.

While there are many ways to invite student voice—through various councils, teams, and clubs—Mr. Porter demonstrated the most important characteristics of all: the willingness to listen, the ability to empathize, and a desire to do what's best for kids.

One of my school leadership mentors had a sign affixed to the wall in his office asking one simple question, "Is it GOOD for KIDS?" This became a mantra of sorts as we discussed various proposals, events, and programs in the schools. When he retired, he left the sign behind so I might continue to make decisions and invite input with that question in mind, and it has been remarked upon by more than one parent and teacher as they enter the office.

Acting on the principle that our basic responsibility is to do what's best for kids rather than what is comfortable for adults is not always easy. Because so many of the issues and concerns that come to school leaders each day are adult issues and concerns, we often lose sight of our purpose. Reminders like the sign in my office help to ground us in the work we need to be doing, and when we act as Mr. Porter did—teaching students valuable lessons about civil discourse and responsibility—we elevate their voice as well as our own profession.

Student-led IEPs

Typically, students receiving special education services are among the least empowered students in schools. While they may be provided with more significant support than other students, that support is often defined by adults, designed by adults, and implemented by adults, with students having little say in the matter.

In some schools, that practice is changing, and students are stepping into the center at Individual Education Plan (IEP) meetings. Following the lead of many schools that implemented student-led conferencing over the past few decades, a number of schools have found value in providing their special needs students with a greater voice in their personal educational programming. This begins with student-led IEP meetings. Rather than the case manager or special education administrator opening the meeting, driving the agenda, and leading the conversation—which directs the focus of the meeting toward them, student-led IEPs result in the student remaining front and center throughout the meeting.

While this may seem awkward or clumsy at first, team members supporting the student report noticeable growth in the student throughout each year, and for those who work with the student over multiple years, the growth is remarkable.

Clearly, the level of student participation in the IEP process will be as individualized as the IEP itself. We should not expect that every student will lead the meeting, but for those who are able, it is an empowering experience. Start by choosing a few students in whom you have confidence that this is something they will enjoy. Provide them with a bit of training as to how the meeting will go, then guide them through the agenda to increase their own comfort level, and you will soon see why this model builds trust among students, families, and staff.

When students trust they are safe and that teachers and school leaders have their best interests at heart, they can perform at their best and demonstrate significant growth each year. This happens most powerfully when trust is pervasive at all layers of the school. When we observe schools performing at levels that exceed expectations, it is likely school leadership has thoughtfully and deliberately taken steps to make student voice, and therefore student trust—a high priority.

For Thought and Discussion

1. Do students feel safe in your schools? How do you know? Is there data you can point to that indicates both their level of safety and their feelings of safety? How might you find out for sure?

2. Is every student in your school known by at least one adult? Does each student have at least one adult they can confide in and seek advice from?

3. How has leadership in your school modeled the importance of strong relationships with students?

4. What structures are in place for amplifying student voice in your schools? Do those structures support a culture of empowerment for students, or are they largely for show?

5. How might you increase student trust in the school? Are there strategies you can employ as an individual and others you can encourage as a leader that will promote engagement between staff and students?

Notes

1 Feldman, J., *Grading for Equity: What It Is, Why It Matters, and How It Can Transform Schools and Classrooms* (Thousand Oaks, CA: Corwin Press, 2018).

2 Porter, Brian, Email to author, February 14, 2025.

10 Family Connections

If you have children of school age, you likely have noticed the metamorphosis that occurs regarding their communication as they progress through the grade levels from primary school through graduation. It's a phenomenon most parents experience when they attempt to stay connected with their kids by asking about the events of the day.

As a kindergartener and early-grade school student, your child likely greeted you each afternoon with an unending description of the things that happened at school that day, without any need for prompting: "Ms. Smith showed us a picture of her puppy!" "We played soccer at recess!" "Annalise fell asleep during story time."

As your child progressed into middle school, you probably had to ask them direct questions to obtain any information about their day, and when asked, "What did you do at school today?" your child likely said, "Nothing." This non-response will be topped only by your child's further regression in high school, when they will typically reply with an inaudible groan or, "I don't want to talk about it!"

As parents, we want to know what is happening at school. Other than home, it is the place where our children spend most of their time and the activities in which they engage—and the relationships formed—are critical to their development and happiness. What happens at school matters—a lot—and parents want to be sure of their children's progress, safety, and comfort when they are at school.

Clearly, the partnership between schools and families is critical, relying on a foundation of mutual trust. When schools and families work together in an atmosphere of trust and respect, students thrive academically, socially, and emotionally.

The importance of this trust cannot be overstated. It acts as a bridge between the two most influential settings in a student's life—home and school. At home, students develop their primary values, beliefs, and behaviors. It's where they first learn about relationships, responsibilities, and the world around them. School, on the other hand, is where students expand their knowledge, develop social skills, and prepare for their future roles in society.

When this bridge is strong, information flows freely, expectations align, and support systems reinforce each other; students receive consistent messages about the value of their education and the importance of acting with integrity. They sense a connection between home and school, and this harmony provides a supportive, stable experience throughout their developmental years.

This alignment is crucial for student success. For example, if both home and school emphasize the importance of effort and perseverance, students are more likely to develop a growth mindset and resilience in facing academic challenges; if a student is working on improving their organizational skills at school, parents who trust and communicate with the school can implement similar strategies at home.

This reinforcement can also extend to celebrating achievements and addressing challenges. When schools and families trust each other, they can coordinate their efforts to provide comprehensive support for the child's academic, social, and emotional needs.

One of the most powerful outcomes of a trusting relationship is the consistency in messages that students receive about the importance of education. When families and schools are aligned in their educational values, students receive clear, unambiguous signals about the value of effort, perseverance, and engagement. This consistency helps to motivate students and gives them a clear sense of purpose in their educational journey. It can also help to mitigate potential conflicts between home and school.

Finally, when there's trust between home and school, students experience a sense of continuity in their daily lives. The transition between home and school becomes smoother, as students feel that both environments are working together for their benefit. This continuity can be particularly important for children facing challenges or changes in their lives. When a family is going through a difficult time, a trusting relationship with the school can ensure that the student receives consistent support and understanding in both settings.

As with any relationship, building and maintaining trust between the school and families requires deliberate effort, open communication, and a willingness to collaborate from both sides. Schools must demonstrate transparency in their policies and decision-making processes, actively seeking family input and involvement while valuing the unique insights families bring to the table. Families must feel welcome to engage with the school and, in turn, participate in their child's education, approaching the school with an open mind.

When schools build trusting relationships with families, the benefits extend far beyond improved academic performance:

- Families are more likely to reinforce school policies and expectations.
- Students feel more secure and supported in their learning environment.
- Teachers can focus more on instruction, with reduced conflicts and misunderstandings.
- Schools enjoy greater community support for innovative practices.

Conversely, when trust is lacking, the consequences can be severe. Miscommunication breeds misunderstanding, leading to conflict and resistance. Students may receive mixed messages about the importance of education, potentially undermining their motivation and achievement. Schools struggle to implement improvements, and families may feel alienated from their children's educational experience.

Parental Involvement

Researchers and practitioners alike agree on the impact of parental involvement on student success. It is not surprising to hear many say that students whose parents are involved in their education tend to have better grades, higher test scores, and better overall academic performance.

Consider the three-legged stool analogy, in which schools, students, and parents each represent a leg supporting the greatest growth of the child. If any leg is weak or disengaged, the student has a tougher balancing act as they attempt to reach their greatest potential. With all three legs solidly in place—along parallel paths and bearing equal responsibility—the student has the best chance for success.

Building and maintaining trust between schools and families is a complex, ongoing process that requires commitment and effort from all parties involved. It's not something that happens automatically or overnight, but rather a relationship that must be cultivated over time.

Schools must prioritize family engagement as a core part of their mission, not just an afterthought. This means allocating resources, time, and staff to family outreach and engagement programs. It might involve creating a dedicated position for family liaison, offering regular workshops for parents, or establishing a family resource center within the school.

Theory in Action

Many schools have taken the approach that they have a responsibility to engage families in meaningful ways outside of the school day, beyond the parameters of the annual Open House or Parent-Teacher Conferences. While each of those events is an important structure to have in place, some additional work can be done to foster a more collaborative approach to educating the students.

One way to do this is to set up what some districts refer to as Parent University, or a Family/School Alliance. During this programming, schools provide learning opportunities for parents through presentations on topics of importance to the community. These programs range from parenting classes that meet on a weekly or monthly basis, to "hot topic" discussions that occur several times each year.

A recent example regards student use of personal technology, which has become a significant concern for many parents and educators. As we have all become more attached to our cellphones and smartwatches, the inclination to scroll through social media and stay in constant contact with others through texting or other digital means has grown exponentially among students. We now see elementary school students wearing smartphones, receiving texts from their friends, or—even more likely—their parents throughout the school day. The distractions and the pressure to stay engaged are well-documented, and many believe they are seeing significant detrimental impacts on student well-being.

In the summer of 2024, a movement took hold throughout the United States, with many schools and families pointing to the data shared by Jonathan Haidt in his book, *The Anxious Generation,* as the bellwether driving a change in policies and practices that would limit student access to smart devices and social media during the school day. The book and its supporters encouraged families and schools to delay and limit student access, especially while at school, and to return to a less digital world in which students engaged—physically, socially, emotionally, and intellectually with one another and the world around them.[1]

This call led many districts to engage with motivated parent groups to offer book talks, panel presentations, and community discussions aimed at better-defining parameters regarding student use of technology. In some districts, the work led to a change in policies and practice almost immediately, as families and the school navigated the tricky waters of balancing student safety (by allowing cell phones to be brought to and from school for parental communication) with student well-being (by limiting access to phones during the day and removing some of the stressors of continual online engagement).

Seeing schools and families working together in this effort to develop strategies that benefit students serves as a motivator for similar work in other areas where common interests might be found. The topics are easily identified:

- growing levels of student anxiety
- increased access to and potency of recreational marijuana
- the pressures of academic overload
- the dangers of vaping and nicotine addiction

Schools would do well to identify topics of significance in their own community and engage knowledgeable professionals who could sit on a panel or facilitate community conversations about those topics. Professionals from the surrounding region are likely to be good resources as you develop your agenda for the evening, and they may be willing to serve as presenters or participants to promote something about which they are passionate.

If you must pay for speakers, and funding is not available through the district budget, consideration should be given to working with a local parent group, like a parent-teacher organization (PTO) or a nonprofit foundation—even a local business may be interested in sponsoring the event. Providing the sponsor with the opportunity to set up a display, hand out pamphlets, or speak for a moment or two at the beginning or end of the event goes a long way toward building support for the schools throughout the community.

Take the time to iron out the details for the event, promoting it through your newsletters, targeted communications, and digital platforms. Ask expected participants to RSVP through electronic means so you can set up the room accordingly, with comfortable seating and proper technology (sound/lights/video). If your first attempt at this work is done well and the topics you select are timely, you will grow your audience for future programs and build greater trust among the families in the district.

Actively Seek Parent Input and Involvement

Beyond simply informing families about events and student progress through typical means, schools should actively seek their input and involvement. This could involve parent surveys before major decisions, focus groups to discuss potential changes, or parent advisory councils that have a real voice in school governance. Schools should also recognize and value the diverse experiences and knowledge that families bring. This might mean inviting parents to share their cultural traditions, professional expertise, or life experiences in the classroom or at school events.

Parent voice on hiring teams—especially for leadership positions—is a critical strategy signifying the school's valuing of parental input. While having a parent on every interview team for teaching positions is not practical, depending on the size of your school, inviting parental participation when hiring principals, assistant principals, and director-level positions should be consistently considered.

Similarly, parental voice should be included on standing or ad-hoc committees with responsibility for policies or programming that will significantly impact student experiences. Ad-hoc groups that benefit from parental input may include, among others:

- strategic planning team
- community partnership committees
- school start time exploration group
- pandemic response task force
- homework policy study group

The topics listed here are examples where we have seen impactful work being done by school leaders, facilitating fairly large groups of constituents—including staff members, elected officials, parents (and sometimes, students)—as they address something as specific as school start times or something as broad-based as the creation of a five-year strategic plan for the district. In each case, inviting parental participation provides an opportunity for school leaders to hear a perspective that is different from that of a school-based employee.

The question is often asked how we can best invite parental input but not be overrun by volunteers. That can be a challenging task, for certain. It is important to clearly define the number of parents you are seeking from each school or grade span prior to seeking volunteers so that when the team is announced, you will have already indicated the number of slots available.

It is also helpful when publishing the team members' names to identify the many ways in which parents who were not selected may still engage with the schools. Whether it be through public forums on the topic at hand, upcoming surveys, or volunteering at the school, you should be able to point out opportunities for parents to support the school so they feel invited, rather than rejected. If possible, a personal note—even by email—goes a long way toward appeasing the volunteers who were not selected.

Take the Call—and Make the Call

It should come as no surprise that one of the most basic forms of trust-building is clear, open communication. What is surprising, though, is how many leaders fail to take advantage of this opportunity when a parent calls (or drops by) the office to make a complaint without forewarning. "Tell them I'm in a meeting," is an all-too-often refrain that places the administrative assistant in the difficult position of having to dismiss the parent or put them into voicemail.

Leaders should not miss out on this opportunity to de-escalate the situation. The voicemail message will likely not be a pleasant one if the parent was already upset when they placed the call and forcing them to express their rage to a machine will do nothing to calm the waters. Similarly, sending them away after they made the effort to drive to the office could only fuel their fire further. On the other hand, the superintendent's voice or presence, asking them how they may be helped, is one of the most consistently effective strategies observed for lowering the temperature.

For your own health, this is good practice, as well. Nobody wants to listen to an irate individual berate them—or one of their employees—by voicemail. Messages like that cause visceral reactions in those toward whom they are directed, and the longer it takes you to respond, the greater the intensity of the caller's displeasure grows.

Make yourself this pledge: If you are available, or if what you are doing can be set aside for a few moments, take the call—and while on the call or in the meeting, remember that the individual's anger or disappointment is not something you need to respond to in kind. Take down the information, express your sincere regrets that something has been communicated to them that has created their disappointment, and tell them you will investigate the matter.

That openness has proven repeatedly to be appreciated by those with whom you are speaking. De-escalation is key to building trust with concerned parents—not in a patronizing way, but in a sincere and candid way. You *are* sorry that this has upset them. You *do* intend to find out the facts and get back to them. You should communicate that to them in a cordial and professional manner without emotion.

More likely than the phone call—in today's world—you are liable to receive an angry email, sent at any and all hours of the night. One simple rule by which to live when it comes to aggressive emails is, *"Do not respond by email."* Instead, just as it's important to *take the call* when someone phones or visits your office, you should *make the call* if you receive a digital communication that expresses displeasure. When you pick up the phone and call the sender, you will almost be guaranteed to disarm them in a way that leaves them much more amenable to your perspective than they would have been had you zipped off an email response.

The one exception to this rule may be when you are in a place where a call cannot be made, and you want to let the individual know that you would be happy to speak with them as soon as possible. In that case, a quick note indicating when you can speak with them to hear more about their concern may be effective.

This sort of attention and willingness to engage on a truly interpersonal level (which email decidedly is *not*) builds trust with the most critical of constituents. Almost nobody expects to receive a telephone call in response to an email. They expect you to respond in kind, and they are likely already preparing their next missive in anticipation of your correspondence. By choosing to speak with them directly, you are demonstrating that you are willing to hear what they have to say, confirming that you are not (a) afraid, (b) defensive, or (c) hiding things.

Clear, consistent, and accessible communication is vital. Schools should utilize multiple channels to reach families through emails, newsletters, social media, phone calls, and face-to-face meetings. Information should be provided in languages spoken by the school community and in formats accessible to all families. The technology is readily available, which allows your communications to be translated for all families. If you don't take that step, you risk losing families who may already feel disconnected from or intimidated by the school. Offering translation services helps to bridge that gap in a more seamless manner.

Building trust is about creating a culture of mutual respect and collaboration. It requires patience, persistence, and a shared commitment to the goal of supporting student success. When both schools and families approach this relationship with dedication and openness, it creates a powerful alliance that can significantly enhance a student's educational experience.

In essence, the trust between schools and families creates an integrated, supportive environment that envelops the student. This environment provides the stability, consistency, and reinforcement necessary for optimal learning and development. It's within this trusting framework that students can truly thrive, feeling secure in the knowledge that the important adults in their lives are working together for their success.

For Thought and Discussion

1. How have you engaged families beyond the traditional Open House and Parent-Teacher Conferences that are standard at many schools? Do you provide evening opportunities for parents/guardians to gather and learn about or discuss topics of importance? Are there other ways for them to interact with the school?

2. What are some topics that might be of interest to families that the school could present? Brainstorm a list and search for themes that might be the basis for a year-long series of parental education programs.

3. How well have you promoted volunteerism as a way for parents to stay connected with schools? What opportunities are offered to parents in this regard, and how are they promoted?

4. How are parents involved in policy and planning for the schools? Do they sit on hiring teams for leadership positions, planning teams, and ad-hoc groups? Identify how they have participated in the past and how they might be engaged in the future.

5. Review your communications systems. How accessible is student information and schoolwide announcements for each parent, regardless of their primary language? Are your digital platforms easily navigable? Ask someone who is not part of your school to find particular items on your website and see how long it takes them to find the information. Some examples they can search for include:
    a. The school calendar
    b. Your daily schedule
    c. Upcoming field trip or concert information
    d. The school principal's name and contact information
    Once you see how others find information on your site, you can better plan how to share information.

Note

1 Haidt, J., *The Anxious Generation: How the Great Rewiring of Childhood Is Causing an Epidemic of Mental Illness* (New York: Penguin Press, 2024).

11 Community Engagement

When we contemplate the importance of trust in our schools, our focus often remains squarely on fostering trust among those with whom we, as school leaders, most frequently interact: teachers, students, and—to a somewhat lesser extent—families. If you are successful in forging authentically trusting relationships with those constituent groups, it is quite likely you will enjoy a long and rewarding career as a school leader.

However, there remains one more group of constituents who look to school leaders for trusted leadership, and who can have a significant and lasting impact on the quality of education offered in each school, and those are the members of the greater community. This includes those members of the public who don't have children in the schools (which, in most communities, is the vast majority of the residents) as well as business owners, alumnae, and others who live or work in the area. These are community leaders, elected officials, and citizens who are also taxpayers and voters. They provide important resources to the school—in the form of financial support, volunteerism, mentoring, and partnerships—and they should not be overlooked.

A strong bond of trust between the school and the community can elevate educational outcomes, strengthen social bonds, and shape the future of entire municipalities. Schools that build a high level of trust with the community contribute significantly toward creating attractive places where alumni return to raise their own families, deepening the trust between school and community and making it a place others want to experience.

There is substantial evidence supporting the idea that when communities trust and support their schools, students enjoy a more positive school climate, are provided with greater resources and opportunities, and perform better academically while learning the importance and value of social cohesion and civic responsibility. Communities that support their schools typically provide significant resources in the form of funding, mentorship programs, and extracurricular activities, all of which enhance educational opportunities and student performance.

Schools do not and cannot operate as isolated institutions; they are integral parts of the communities they serve. When a strong foundation of trust exists, schools become more than just places of learning—they become the center of the community, a source of pride for all within their borders, and vehicles of social progress. Overall, the evidence suggests that a supportive and engaged community plays a crucial role in enhancing educational experiences and academic performance for students.

Building this trust is no simple task. It requires sustained effort, open dialogue, and a willingness to collaborate with all stakeholders. Schools must demonstrate transparency, responsiveness, and a genuine commitment to serving the diverse needs of their community. Community members, in turn, must engage with schools, support the school's efforts, and contribute their unique perspectives and resources. This can only happen when they are welcomed—and beyond that, invited—into the schools as volunteers, mentors, and partners.

Conversely, when trust is lacking, the consequences can be severe. Schools may struggle with declining enrollment, reduced funding, and limited community support. Students may miss out on valuable community resources and real-world learning opportunities, leading to declining academic performance. The community itself may suffer from a diminished sense of identity and reduced social capital, along with lower property values and a lack of investment on all fronts.

By investing in the relationship between schools and communities, we do more than improve educational outcomes—we strengthen the very fabric of our society. Strong, trust-based partnerships between schools and communities create a dynamic cycle of engagement, support, and success that can transform lives and shape the future of entire generations.

Theory in Action

Heather Perry is the Superintendent of Schools in Gorham, Maine—a 3,000-student public school district serving PreK-Grade 12 students in the single municipality of Gorham, located 5 miles outside of Portland, Maine.[1] Gorham is home to the University of Southern Maine and is a community that has enjoyed a reputation for high-quality schools for many decades.

In 2011, business and school leaders in town formed the Gorham Business-Schools Roundtable to explore and foster relationships and communication between the schools and businesses in town and find ways for students to be exposed to career pathways.

The Roundtable typically meets once each academic quarter to explore partnership opportunities for the schools and local businesses to expose students to a variety of career options. While the main focus is on supporting students as they decide on their unique pathway to employment, the Roundtable also supports employers, providing a space for business leaders to discuss their needs with educators who are preparing the next generation of employees.

"The roundtable has been a mainstay in the Gorham community for 14-plus years now, building strong and trusting relationships between our schools and our community business partners—the ultimate goal of which is to work together to expose students to career opportunities and pathways in order to best prepare our students for their successful futures," said Heather.

Through mentorships, internships, classroom presentations, and a variety of special programming, the Roundtable promotes community cohesion, with students becoming more familiar with local businesses and business leaders learning more about the school's challenges and opportunities. An added benefit that is assumed but that has not yet been quantified is the greater likelihood of graduates remaining in—or returning to—the town because of the strong bonds that are formed during their formative years.

Heather adds,

> *The relationships built between business leaders and our schools through the roundtable are strong. The experiences they provide for our students can't be matched, and so our learning programs are strengthened. From the business perspective, this is the future workforce they are investing in, and they'll be able to reap the rewards not too far down the road. I can't think of a better "win-win" partnership for our community.*

Early in her superintendency in Gorham, Heather realized that general support for and engagement with the schools was favorable, but the focus was largely on students following the "traditional" path to graduation. Students who were pursuing Career and Technical Education (CTE) programs at nearby regional vocational schools were negatively stigmatized, making it difficult to enroll students who would benefit most from such programming. This was a problem she communicated to the Business-Schools Roundtable.

In 2017, an idea was hatched at the Roundtable, initiating the Aspire Gorham program. Funding was secured through two different grants, as well as the district's annual operating budget, supporting two full-time positions, with significant funds for field experiences and other work aimed at removing the CTE stigma by exposing students to career exploration experiences and discussions from an early age. Through the Aspire program, students are encouraged to recognize that they each are on a unique path—none less deserving of recognition than any other—opening the door for greater consideration of the options before each student.

"The program's focus is to build the topic of aspirations into *everything* that we do across grades PK-12 and beyond, establishing partnerships with Early Childhood Education and with Adult Education, postsecondary education, and area business leaders," Heather says.

> *In order to be successful, community engagement is needed at each grade level. In PreK through Grade 5, students are exposed to field experience, guest speakers, and the exploration of aspirations throughout the curriculum. Career exploration in grades 6–9 includes activities like "Try it" days, the amazing race, or partnerships with organizations such as Junior Achievement. Finally, experiences in grades 10–12 focus on Extended Learning Opportunities (ELOs) and CTE programs, (Internships, Apprenticeships, and Dual Enrollments).*

Heather added, "All of this is focused on helping students create their future stories knowing that life's trajectories are never in a straight line and that we are always writing chapters!"

Anecdotal evidence from students, staff, families, and business partners indicates that the program is having its desired effect on students. A broader acceptance of the need for individualized pathways, and the value of each of those pathways, appears to be developing. Similarly, more tangible data suggests a high level of trust in the community and positive outcomes for kids:

- Recruitment of over 90 business partners in the local community
- Awarding of over 200 Career Exploration badges to graduating seniors
- Awarding of over 1,600 dual enrollment credits to high school students
- Creation of a public Pre-K program
- Partnership with the local community library, serving over 600 preschool-aged youth in the community.

A couple of significant points can be gleaned from Gorham's experience. First and foremost, the collaboration between schools and businesses has had a positive result for students. More students are selecting appropriately unique pathways, rather than feeling forced into either a fully traditional or a fully CTE mold. This provides for higher levels of satisfaction with school, which leads to greater student engagement and stronger academic outcomes.

Second, the creation of the Business-Schools Roundtable has had a noticeable impact on the relationship between the school and the community. Prior to the Roundtable, interactions were haphazard and random. Over the years, it has become one of structured collaboration, with business and school leaders joining together to identify challenges and propose solutions that call for partnerships and community buy-in.

Doing the Work

Community engagement with schools requires concentrated and consistent effort like that demonstrated in Gorham. Unfortunately, school security measures and the closing of facilities during the Covid-19 pandemic have necessarily forced schools to appear less welcoming, with locked doors, hardened entry points, and background checks for all visitors. There is no doubt this has left some from the community less likely to engage with the schools.

Fortunately, while in-person connections have become more challenging, opportunities for digital communication have expanded rapidly, and school leaders should make use of every available avenue for promoting student progress and successes, highlighting organizational performance, and announcing school events.

Because a large percentage of the community population no longer has direct ties to the schools, many individuals can easily become suspicious or critical of the school. We have all heard the frequent refrains:

- "Why don't they teach *that* (pick your topic) anymore?"
- "When I was in school, things were *different* (read, *better*)."
- "These kids have it so easy nowadays!"

When we expose these naysayers to the work being done by students and staff, debunking the myth that things have gone horribly wrong in recent decades, we create a new generation of supportive community members.

Rather than simply announcing an event that is open to the public—such as a concert, an exhibition, or a contest—schools should consider sending targeted invitations to specific individuals or locations, such as elderly communities, nursing homes, and local business organizations (e.g., chamber of commerce). You may even work with your transportation division to offer a ride to those for whom traveling is difficult. A field trip to a local school performance can be as exciting for some residents as it is for the youngsters who will be on stage.

Another option that has proven successful is to offer reduced ticket prices—or even free admission—to school events for residents of a certain age. Typically, exposing more people to student performances only results in greater support for the schools. Costly ticket prices or travel difficulties cause some to avoid attending and contribute to their sense of disconnectedness from the schools.

While inviting the public into the school—and offering rides and more affordable admission—may encourage engagement for some, the additional step of sending students out into the community in a variety of ways can generate even greater trust in the schools. Field trips to local businesses or historic sites, internships for older students, and primary source interviews to learn more about the experiences of those living in our midst are all important steps to take.

Additionally, student engagement beyond the school grounds—such as mini-concerts at a local business event, gift-giving or craft-making at the local nursing home, and student participation in community boards—connects community members with the schools in tangible, uplifting ways.

While many school districts offer School Board seats to one or two students, opportunities should not be missed for students to sit on community boards, such as Town Council, Climate Action Teams, and other municipal-based groups. Connecting leaders of student clubs with community groups that have a similar focus is a great way to form bonds between the school and community that foster trust and collaboration.

Trusted Financial Management

Of course, one of the most significant opportunities to build trust with the community is presented through the annual budget development process. While the legal requirements for budget development vary from state to state, there is no doubt that concerns around the cost of education continue to drive much of the distrust that is felt by local school leaders.

Regardless of the budget development process you follow, being transparent about that process and sharing copious amounts of accurate data through widespread dissemination of proposals, providing multiple opportunities for community input, and widely publicizing public deliberations by the decision-makers are critical steps to take to prevent misinformation and distrust from sidetracking your budget.

Budget outreach takes many forms, which can be categorized in one of three ways:

- Passive
- Active—Canvased
- Active—Targeted

Through passive outreach, schools place informative documents in places where interested constituents are likely to look. Most notably, printed handouts detailing the budget process or proposal can be placed at schools, municipal buildings, or other public locations, while digital versions are posted to an easily identified page on the district website. This digital information should never be more than three clicks from the main page, following an intuitive path that leads the viewer from the main page to the school finance page to the proposed budget page.

You can test this by asking a colleague, friend, or family member to see how long it takes to locate your school's budget information on your website. If they find it confusing or laborious, work with your technology staff to make the information more easily accessible.

The information presented in either of these formats (hard copy or digital) should include data that provides the reader with a clear explanation of the requested adjustments to the budget. A good list from which to begin includes year-over-year comparisons for:

- Student enrollment—by school and by grade
- Class size reports—with comparisons to district or state guidelines
- Per pupil expenditures—with comparisons to local districts and the state average
- Student needs—including data for special education, ADA Section 504, Multi-lingual learners, Gifted & Talented, etc.
- Impact of any state laws or funding changes
- Student performance data—including graduation rates, state/national testing results, attendance data, etc.

Once the proposed budget is developed, this data can be arranged as both a narrative and a slide deck, both of which should be distributed and posted in hard copy and digital formats. One additional piece that should be added to the website and offered to citizens on an as-requested basis is the line-item budget. While this is likely too lengthy to print for every resident, making it available digitally is further evidence of the district's willingness to share all information in a transparent manner.

A final item that can be shared publicly is a video presentation and explanation of the proposed budget. When done well, the superintendent's explanation of the budget—touching upon the data mentioned throughout the budget narrative—indicates a commitment to understanding the budget and a willingness to present the data in a manner that is understandable to the average citizen.

One of the benefits of this strategy is that the information can be updated and remain on the website for the entire academic year—and warehoused as it becomes "prior year" data. When community members are confident that the information they are seeking is readily available and they have the capability to look at prior years to see how things have changed, they become less likely to accuse you of hiding things from them and more likely to appreciate the access you have provided.

In the Active–Canvased category are the same items presented in the Passive category, distributed to families and residents by email, hard copy, newsletters, and local newspapers. By sending these documents directly to listservs or announcing their availability in local papers, schools reach many more people than those who take it upon themselves to search for information on the district website. Sending reminders of upcoming meetings, with updated budget information, keeps the public informed of the process at each step.

Finally, in the Active–Targeted category are those presentations school leaders make directly to specific individuals or groups to build support for the schools through transparent, face-to-face communication. This may include a presentation to the local PTO, Rotary Club, or Chamber of Commerce. This level of engagement is one of the most effective ways to build trust with constituents who may not be closely associated with the schools. Demonstrating your understanding of both the fiscal and the academic side of the schoolhouse builds confidence in those who may not interact regularly with school leaders.

It is often said, "Communities get the schools they deserve." While this may seem harsh, it is likely an accurate statement. When communities make significant investments in their schools (on a variety of fronts—not just financial), those schools perform at a high level. Conversely, when communities are disengaged and unsupportive, school culture and performance suffer. The willingness to invest is directly related to the level of trust the community has in the school. When trust is high, investments are more likely to be made, and resources for the school are plentiful, leading to greater satisfaction at school, greater aspirations, and stronger performance for both students and teachers.

School leaders play a pivotal role in fostering community trust, investment, and engagement in the schools. Concentrated, consistent efforts like those in Gorham provide examples for others to follow to create meaningful change in how the community views the schools.

In the following chapters, we will explore how deliberate long-term and short-term planning creates a shared vision for the school, generating confidence and promoting collaboration that, combined with the strategies shared earlier, results in a level of trust that ensures the community does, indeed, get the school it deserves.

For Thought and Discussion
1. List the community groups with which you have interacted as a school leader in the past year. How might you lengthen this list in the coming year?
2. How do community leaders know what is going on in your schools? How do you inform them of activities or invite them to participate in school events?
3. What resources exist in your community that could be important connections for students? Think about primary sources of information, mentors and coaches, experts, artists, and entrepreneurs who might provide students with amazing experiences that inspire them to think differently about school and the world around them.
4. How well are you preparing your students for their next phase? What data can you point to that indicates your success in this area? Do we know what skills and knowledge they will need in their first year of schooling or work beyond high school?
5. How do your students explore careers and learn about the opportunities they may have in the future? Are you providing enough in this area? What are the challenges getting in the way, and how might you get past them?

Note

1   Perry, Heather, Email to author, May 13, 2024.

12 Strategic Planning
Preparing to Plan

Note: Chapters 12 and 13 provide a detailed guide for school leaders to consider when constructing a strategic plan for the district. If your schools already have a solid comprehensive plan in place, you may want to skip these chapters for now, coming back to them when the time to develop a new plan has arrived. Moving ahead to Chapter 14 will provide you with ideas for ensuring your plan is a living document that drives decision-making for your organization.

Private sector organizations have long understood the need for a well-crafted, outcome-oriented strategic plan to guide their work. In recent decades, schools have followed suit, with the highest-performing districts working collaboratively with community partners to develop clearly articulated plans that identify the school's mission and core values along with well-defined goals, action strategies, and performance measures. With such a plan in place, the school can focus its work on achieving the mission, garnering community support for the strategies identified, and aligning resources to implement the plan.

Much has been written on the importance of strategic planning, and most authors and researchers agree that a well-crafted strategic plan provides the following benefits:

- Articulates a collaboratively developed mission, vision, and core values
- Identifies how success is defined, including performance metrics
- Reduces conflict while promoting cohesiveness
- Informs decision-making
- Improves communication and collaboration

- Provides a framework for school improvement focused on student outcomes

It is easy to assume that schools can operate without a clearly articulated strategic plan. After all, it's quite evident that the vast majority of educators enter the profession with a fairly similar understanding of what schooling is about. Shouldn't we, therefore, be able to operate our schools with an unstated "common understanding" of what we're trying to accomplish?

That is exactly the approach I took for the early part of my own leadership career, and while our school made some significant progress due to a talented and dedicated professional staff and a community that demonstrated strong support for its schools, looking back a few decades later, I can say that my leadership could have been more clearly focused had we adopted a collaboratively developed mission statement—with corresponding core values—that led to a strategic plan for improving the school. Without that plan, it was the leadership team's vision (or the topic of the day) that was driving decision-making by default, with nothing for the staff, students, and community to grasp onto and say, "This is what we're about; this is what we're trying to accomplish, and this is how we're going to get there."

Fortunately, we had a strong leadership team in place at the school, with a good blend of experienced and newer staff members, who were fully engaged in the decision-making process. Discussions around budgeting, curriculum, program development, and student expectations were robust and purposeful. Still, I wonder now how much greater our improvement would have been had we started with the development of a strategic plan rather than taking each year as it came to us and responding to needs reactively rather than proactively.

Schools that operate without a strategic plan risk a muddled approach to program assessment and development, risking confusion, mixed messaging, and—eventually—disengagement. With a thoughtful plan in place—one that allows for nimble flexibility when unforeseen challenges arise (e.g., a global pandemic)—schools foster trust from the community by publicly declaring their goals and sharing how they will approach the work and measure their success.

Developing a strategic plan for your school or district can seem a daunting task. The last thing anyone needs is a string of lengthy meetings at which nothing is accomplished and after which everyone leaves feeling frustrated.

This happens frequently in strategic planning because it seems like a "black box" activity that nobody really understands.

It is possible to reduce confusion, nurture engagement, and simplify the planning process by identifying the components of strategic planning, breaking them down into phases, and developing a planning schedule for the year. In so doing, the school leader can drive the planning process forward in an effective and efficient manner, resulting in the creation of a long-term plan in one year or less.

Essentially, the phases of strategic planning include:

- Pre-Planning
- Launching
- Assessment
- Goal Setting
- Planning
- Presenting & Refining
- Approval & Dissemination
- Operationalizing
- Promotion & Implementation

We will look at each of these phases in more detail to help guide your district through the planning process, whether it is for the first time or in a setting where a strategic plan is being refreshed.

Phase 1: Pre-planning

Team Formation and Charge

During the pre-planning phase, a school has already determined that it must adopt or refresh a strategic plan. The district may have a plan that is expiring—or has recently expired—or it may not have had a plan in place in recent years. Either way, the development of a new plan is desired. At this point, it is important for school leadership to answer several questions that will have a great bearing on the effectiveness of the planning process:

How Will the Process Be Facilitated?

There are various approaches to facilitation available to schools as they go through the planning process, but the most common are:

- Internal facilitation
- Consultant-informed facilitation, and
- Consultant-driven facilitation

Internal facilitation occurs when a district elects to conduct the entire planning process with no outside consultation. This may be the method of choice when a district is very tight on funding and/or the leadership team (administration and School Board) feels highly confident that they have the right person or persons in place to guide this important work. This approach can be highly effective for districts in which the school leadership has credibility with staff and the community.

The benefits of internal facilitation include that it is less expensive than hiring consultants, it provides opportunities for trust-building between school leadership and the community, and it allows school leaders to demonstrate their willingness to engage in the hard work of collaborative decision-making with staff and other constituents.

One downside to internal facilitation is that it may appear to some constituents that the school is adopting an internal approach in order to control the narrative and avoid being challenged to adopt loftier goals. Another potential downside is if the chosen leader has overestimated their own facilitation skills or is deficient in their willingness to collaborate, leading to greater mistrust when people are left to ask, "Was that what we decided? I don't remember it that way!"

Schools that choose the internal facilitation process should do so only when the entire team making the decision (including representatives of school-based leadership and Board leadership) is 100 percent confident they have the right person in place to lead the process, and the climate in the school and community is conducive to a locally led process. With an engaging, expert school leader at the helm—one who is willing to listen and assist others in framing their ideas—an internal process can be a wonderfully rewarding experience that results in a widely praised plan for the school.

At the opposite end of the planning spectrum is the consultant-driven process. This occurs when the school hires an outside individual or organization to oversee the process, including the facilitation of meetings, forums, surveys, and other planning tasks.

The upside of a consultant-driven process is that the school recognizes its own lack of experience in this area, bringing on board individuals with a wealth of knowledge who have developed approaches to the work that have been honed through years of working in community development. These professionals may bring with them exemplars from prior engagements, helping the school avoid the pitfalls that may have tripped up their colleagues in other schools.

The downside of consultant-driven planning is threefold. First, it can be very expensive, which is always a consideration for schools. When school leaders are attempting to build trust with their communities, expending tens of thousands of dollars on outside consultants is not a practice to be undertaken frequently or lightly.

A second negative aspect of consultant-driven planning is that, typically, these consultants come from outside the community. Therefore, there can be a level of distrust and concern that they don't know the community or that they will attempt to guide the work toward a "cookie-cutter" plan that has worked well elsewhere. Schools that adopt a consultant-led process will need to be cautious to ensure the plan is truly individualized for their community, rather than allowing consultants to adopt a plan that would be better suited elsewhere.

Finally, the most noticeable negative aspect of consultant-driven planning is that the school leader is missing an opportunity to stand in front of and alongside the staff and community and demonstrate their facilitation skills, concern for the schools, and overall leadership abilities. These are opportunities that should be capitalized upon, if possible. Effective facilitation of staff feedback loops, public forums, and planning team meetings are prime opportunities for trust-building between the leader and the wider community.

This leads us then to the consultant-informed model, which many schools have found to be the perfect balance between the "do-it yourself" model of internal facilitation and the "call in the experts" model of the consultant-driven process. In the consultant-informed model, the district engages the services of an experienced strategic planning expert, who advises the leadership team while relying heavily upon the resources within the school to oversee the facilitation of meetings and the driving of the planning process. The benefits of this model are significant; the school can rely on expert advice and learn from the experiences of others while retaining ownership of the process and demonstrating the leadership skills of their own team, all while developing a plan for much less money than the consultant-driven model.

The only downside to the consultant-informed model is that the school will spend money that it would not spend when facilitating the process internally. Again, for districts with an inexperienced leadership team, this may be a small price to pay if it leads to the development of an effective plan while providing the school leader with valuable facilitation experience that deepens the trust they share with the community.

Once the facilitation model is decided upon, the pre-planning phase continues with the consideration of how others will be engaged in the process—identified in questions 2 and 3.

Who Will Be Engaged at the Executive Level of the Planning Process?

It is critically important for the planning team to be of adequate size to include a range of constituents while also being small enough to be an effective working group. Evan Wittenberg, director of the Wharton Graduate Leadership Program, notes that team size is "not necessarily an issue people think about immediately, but it is important." According to Wittenberg, while the research on optimal team numbers is not conclusive, it does tend to fall into the five to twelve range, though some say five to nine is best.[1]

It is highly unlikely that a group of five to nine people will be large enough to represent the many constituents who will want to be engaged in the planning process. At the same time, groups of fifteen to twenty or more are typically too large to accomplish anything efficiently. Therefore, the leadership team must be thoughtful in determining the constituent groups that will be represented at the planning table.

You should keep the number tight while seeking the broadest representation possible. This may be accomplished by looking at the duality of roles—such as a parent who is also a business owner or a teacher who is also a resident—while considering how each candidate represents different sectors of the community. If you can keep the planning team to twelve members (no more than fifteen) you will be able to move the work forward while also recognizing varied perspectives.

At this point, the school's leadership should list specifically which constituent groups will be represented on the planning team. Those to be considered often include:

- Teachers/Staff members
- Administrators
- Board members
- Parents
- Other elected officials/community leaders
- Business owners
- Students

A comprehensive and well-defined list should be developed and adopted by the Board, with a plan for determining how candidates will be invited to volunteer for—and selected to—the team. While a lottery system may be the fairest way to select the members, schools should not dismiss the idea of selecting members from the candidate pool based on their ability to serve in a duality of roles, as mentioned above.

What Will the Charge of the Planning Team Be, and Who Will Have the Authority to Edit, Adopt, and Distribute the Plan?

One of the surest ways to degrade trust in leadership is to mislead others into thinking they have authority and, at the end of the day, dismiss their input. This is why it is vitally important that the leadership of the school be very clear at the outset of the planning process as to who will be involved, what their responsibilities will be, and how much authority they will have in the adoption of the final product.

Because the School Board is the publicly elected or appointed group tasked with overseeing the operation of the schools, they should retain the authority to edit and adopt the strategic plan in its final format. While the planning team itself is tasked with doing research, engaging the community and staff, and drafting the plan, the Board and superintendent should make clear from the outset the parameters within which the planning team will work.

To do this most effectively—and with transparency—at this stage in the process the Board should craft and adopt a charge to be given to the planning team. This charge should be presented at a regular meeting of the Board, with a formal vote taken to form and charge the group with developing the plan.

The charge should include:

- the desired composition of the team
- a list of required components of the plan
- a call for the engagement of the community
- a timeline for completion of the draft plan.

Finally, the charge must delineate where the planning team's authority ends and the Board's authority begins. A sample charge is provided in Table 12.1 for consideration.

School leaders should adopt a charge such as this to meet the needs of their own community. Because each community is unique, with its own formal and informal organizational structures, it is important for leadership to thoughtfully determine the composition of the planning team to maximize perspectives while maintaining an appropriately sized working group. Searching for individuals who can serve multiple roles and identifying the roles they fill will help to legitimize their selection.

Table 12.1 Sample School Board Charge to the Strategic Planning Team

A strategic planning team will be formed by (insert date) to create a proposed five-year strategic plan for the school district to include, at a minimum, statements of mission and core beliefs, with identified goals, performance measures, and suggested actions to be taken for meeting those goals.
The team will be composed of: • Two members of the School Board • One member of the City Council • Three school administrators • Three teachers • One high school student • Two community members • Superintendent of Schools
The planning team will engage the community and staff in the planning process through public forums, staff feedback loops, and/or surveys, will report on its progress at a School Board meeting each month, and will present a draft plan for the School Board's review, input, and eventual approval by the final School Board meeting of the school year. The School Board reserves the authority to edit, approve, and distribute the Strategic Plan.

Once the team is formed, an announcement should be made to the community, introducing the team—along with the charge adopted by the School Board. The announcement may also provide the schedule of planning team meetings if known at that time.

An important consideration will be how to introduce each member of the planning team in the community announcement. If you have chosen well, several members of the Team will be able to represent more than one of the roles defined by the School Board charge, and their place on the Team should not be confined to a singular characteristic.

As an example, let's say Francine is selected to serve on the planning team as a City Councilor. She is also the parent of two students in the district and a business owner in town. When publicizing the list of planning team members, each of Francine's roles should be listed. Doing this for each member of the planning team will indicate to the community the thoughtful approach taken by the leadership in forming the team and will help to communicate the broad perspectives that are represented by the group.

What Will the Timeline Be for Adoption of the Plan?

"Planning backward" is a popular phrase when taking on a complex, long-term project in any organization, and it is one for which strategic planning is well-suited. Identifying the date by which you will want to finalize the plan will allow the creation of a timeline that identifies critical points along the way.

Although a plan may be finalized at any point in the year, it seems logical to aim for a late spring or early summer adoption by the School Board, thereby providing the leadership team with several months to operationalize the plan (to be discussed later) and develop a plan for distribution and promotion prior to the start of the school year. Kicking off a new academic year with the unveiling of the newly adopted—or reaffirmed—mission statement and core values can be an energizing way to welcome staff and students back to school. Similarly, onboarding new staff with a freshly adopted plan is an engaging approach to an orientation that promotes cohesiveness and singularity of purpose.

With an adoption date selected, you can begin planning backward from that point. Assume it will take eight to ten meetings of the full planning team, along with three or four meetings for sub-groups, two rounds of community and staff input, and a community-wide survey. With concentrated effort and strong guidance from school leadership, all of this can be done in approximately ten months, though it may take longer in some settings. Once you have read through the suggested steps in this chapter and those to follow, you'll be ready to plan backward and set up your benchmark events to drive your planning calendar.

Creating the Timeline

After the charge is developed and the team is formed, school leadership should develop the proposed timeline and begin the early stages of data collection—a critically important pre-planning step that will serve as a foundation for the Planning team's understanding of the district's characteristics and performance. The sample timeline in Table 12.2 identifies the dates of the team meetings and the tasks to be scheduled to complete the planning process in one year.

While it is important to lay out this schedule for the year, it is also important to remain flexible and understand that not every meeting will go according to plan. This timeline is simply a roadmap for completing the work and arriving at your destination if no obstacles or detours exist, but that is unlikely. Your ability to keep things moving forward while addressing those bumps in the road along the way will be a major factor in the team's success in finalizing the plan within the time provided.

Data Collection

Performance and Demographic Data

As soon as a school or district determines that it will be engaging in the strategic planning process, the administration should begin to identify, collect, and collate data that will help the organization define "Who we are" and, subsequently, "Who we want to be" and "How we will measure our progress." This work should occur concurrently with the development of the charge and the formation of the planning team so that once the team is formed, up-to-date data is ready to be shared to assist each member in understanding the school's current performance, successes, and challenges.

Table 12.2 Timeline and Planning Process

LAUNCH

October Planning team (PT) Meeting 1—

- Receive charge from SC
- Review timeline and process
- Review sample plans from schools across the United States

November PT Meeting 2

- Share thoughts of plan review from other schools
- Discuss preferred components for plan
- Develop Action Team for each potential component
- Begin review of Mission and Core Beliefs
- Plan Community Forum

ASSESS

Nov—Dec. Staff Feedback Loop I

- Superintendent will facilitate faculty/staff discussions

December Community Forum I

- Introduce process
- SAU data; "Who we are"
- SWOT input
- Response to current Mission and Core Beliefs
- "Who we want to be"
- Next Steps

December PT Meeting 3

- Review input from Community Forum and Staff Feedback Loop
- Propose Mission and Core Beliefs edits
- Develop Achievement Vision
- Assign Action Team tasks
- Create vision statement for Action Area
- Create three to five action strategies for Action Area

GOAL SETTING

January PT Meeting 4

- Review Mission and Core Beliefs progress
- Review Achievement Vision progress
- Action Team report out and feedback

PLAN

February PT Meeting 5

- Finalize draft of Mission and Core Beliefs
- Finalize draft of Achievement Vision
- Continue Action Team report out and feedback

March PT Meeting 6

- Finalize draft of Action Areas

PRESENT & REFINE

March PT Meeting 7

- Review finalized draft for presentation at Community Forum II
- Plan Community Forum II

March Staff Feedback Loop II
April Community Forum II

- Present draft of Strategic Plan
- Provide format for individual and group feedback

April PT Meeting 8

- Review input from Community Forum and Staff Feedback Loop
- Suggest edits to draft

April PT Meeting 9

- Review appendices and support data presented by administration
- Prepare for presentation to SC

May School Board (SB) Meeting 1

- Receive draft of Strategic Plan

APPROVE & DISSEMINATE

May SB Meeting 2

- Approve final draft of Strategic Plan

OPERATIONALIZE

June Leadership Team develops Action Strategy template and promotes mission, core values, and plan throughout the organization.

PROMOTE & IMPLEMENT

Fall Leadership Team works with staff at each school to begin implementation of the plan

While much is made of standardized test scores, seasoned educators know this is not the only data that defines a school's position in the community. Along with academic performance and attendance data, schools should consider student, staff, and community demographics, faculty qualifications, and district expenditures as potential data points to help them understand and define the school's characteristics and efficiencies. Table 12.3 provides a non-exhaustive list of possible data to be collected.

To provide a more comprehensive view of the district's characteristics and performance, districts should present three- and five-year data at a minimum and consider comparisons with national, state, and local data.

The collection of data is just the first step in this process. For the planning team to work most efficiently, the district should task one talented individual with organizing the pertinent data into charts, graphs, and/or tables that are attractive and easy to understand. This represents a tremendous amount of work, but front-loading the effort in this way will make the work of the

Table 12.3 Potential Data Points

Students	Staff	District
Demographics*	Demographics	Demographics
Achievement	Qualifications	Per pupil expenditures
• State testing	Education	Other budget data (% spend, etc.)
• Graduation rates	Experience	Local vs. state/federal aid
• College-going rates		
• Career-ready measures		
• SAT/ACT scores		
• Advanced placement		
• International baccalaureate		
• Universal screeners		
Attendance		
Health & wellness		
• Survey data		
• Social work data		
• School health data		

*Demographics may include SES (income), ancestry, race, special education, 504, age, etc.

planning team much easier, as they will have the data they need to have shared with them in an efficient manner.

Sample Plans

It is difficult to imagine creating from scratch an appropriate strategic plan for an organization as large and complex as a school district. What should the components of such a plan be? How will we ensure we don't miss anything?

Fortunately, this is not a wheel you need to recreate in a vacuum. Thousands of school district strategic plans have been created over the past few decades, and most of them are easily accessible in digital format—all we need to do is spend some time looking, and we can find plenty of examples to stimulate our minds and inspire our best work.

While it is easy to look to our closest neighbors for comparisons, it is also important to look for samples from other regions of the country and even internationally if we are to stretch our thinking and challenge our local schools to be leaders on a larger stage. And why shouldn't we want this? We have to believe that our mission is as important as that of any school in the world—and our students are as capable as those at any school in the world—so we should look globally for model plans that challenge us to define appropriate, aspirational goals for our schools.

When collecting sample plans, it is best to set up a digital folder and provide links to electronic versions of each plan, offering team members the opportunity to add to the file plans from schools/districts with which they are familiar, or that they have found on their own. In this way, you are setting the stage early in the process for welcoming input from team members and demonstrating openness to varying perspectives.

With the team formed, the timeline in place, and data collection underway, the planning process can begin in earnest. In the following chapters, we'll look at a step-by-step process for ensuring the process is efficient, yet comprehensive. Just as with the timeline, oversight of the entire planning process must allow for flexibility; the process proposed here simply provides a framework that should be modified to meet the needs of your district.

For Thought and Discussion

1. Where is your strategic plan located? Can anyone easily find it on your website? Is it available in hard copy at each school or office?

2. How frequently do you refer to the strategic plan throughout the school year? Is it driving the work of the schools each year? Are there measurable targets and actions you and your team are striving to meet?

3. How important is it for you to be the face of the district when leading the planning process? Are you comfortable leading this work, or will you need some guidance from a planning consultant?

4. Identify the data you will use to characterize your district as you begin the planning process. What data points are important to the school and community?

5. Think about who should be represented on your planning team. Can you keep the number of participants manageable while also ensuring solid representation of constituents? Develop a list of roles you will want represented on your team.

Note

1 Knowledge at Wharton Staff, "Is Your Team Too Big? Too Small? What's the Right Number?" (June 2006), https://knowledge.wharton.upenn.edu/podcast/knowledge-at-wharton-podcast/is-your-team-too-big-too-small-whats-the-right-number-2/.

13 Strategic Planning
Creating the Plan

With the team in place and data collection underway, you are ready to begin holding planning meetings. As with any task of this magnitude, meeting preparation is critical to the team's effectiveness. You should hold your first planning team meeting once a significant amount of data is collected and organized for easy consumption. Postponing the first meeting so you can hit the ground running in a more organized fashion is far better than stumbling out of the gate during the launch phase.

As you prepare to host your first meeting you should work out a plan for keeping a record of all meetings, forums, and feedback loops. This record will include the names of everyone who attended each planning meeting and any decisions that were made. Minutes of each meeting do not need to be a transcript of everything that was said, nor do they need to include every proposal that was discussed. Keeping a record simply of who was there and the decisions that were made—with any assignments and upcoming events/meetings noted—will be important as you present your product later on in the process. For larger meetings (public forums, faculty feedback loops, etc.) you need not list the names of everyone present, but it is a good idea to note how many attended each, as it helps to legitimize your work as a collaborative effort.

You will also need to determine at this point how you will keep the public apprised of your work. One easy step to take is the creation of a webpage linked to your district's website. Here you can post the planning team's charge, along with the meeting schedule and minutes of meetings as they occur. Providing a list of team members with email addresses at which they may be reached is another strategy for inviting input. News articles on the front page of the district website, along with periodic reports from the planning team or superintendent at public Board meetings, are two popular methods for keeping this work visible for the community.

One of the first agenda items will be to share the meeting schedule for the year. Rather than spending time at the end of each meeting attempting to coordinate the schedules of ten to fifteen team members you can publish the schedule for the entire year and address any problematic dates that may need to be moved. By sharing a timeline for the year similar to the sample provided in Chapter 12, team members will be able to adjust their schedules accordingly, committing to the schedule as presented—or you can consider rearranging a few of the meetings if they conflict with a significant number of team members' schedules. Either way, setting the schedule for the year gives everyone the chance to block out those times in their respective calendars.

Monthly or bimonthly monthly meetings should suffice for the full team. Let your team members know that there will likely be a need for smaller working groups to meet outside of the full team meetings later in the process, but those can be scheduled by individual groups when the time comes.

In addition to providing advance notice of meetings by presenting the year-long schedule, you should consider setting not just a start time but also an end time for each meeting. Most groups lose steam after ninety minutes, so with diminishing returns after that point, it is good to set that as an agreed-upon parameter for your meetings. Not only does this prevent meetings from dragging on for hours on end, but it also keeps the group focused, knowing that they have much to accomplish in those ninety minutes at each meeting.

To work efficiently, "piggybacking" of meetings has been successful in some settings. For example, a district may schedule planning team meetings on the same evening as a regular School Board meeting, starting two hours earlier and thereby limiting the number of nights Board members and school leaders must be out each month. This approach also provides time for the ninety-minute meeting parameter, with a thirty-minute break between the end of the planning meeting and the start of the Board meeting.

Phase 2: Launch

With a meeting schedule prepared, the team is ready to begin its work, starting with the "Launch" phase of this important project. A successful launch is critical for building positive momentum at the beginning of the process. You want members to leave the first meeting feeling energized, empowered, and confident that they understand what the planning process will look like, what their role will be, and what they need to do in preparation for the next meeting. A sample agenda for the team's first meeting is shared in Table 13.1.

It is important to review the charge from the School Board at the very beginning of the process, and it will likely need to be reiterated as the planning team works throughout the year. Most importantly, point out that the Board has identified the required components of the plan and that the Board will have final editing and approval authority for the plan. It is critical at this juncture for the team to know the extent of its authority, which is the development of a proposed plan, not the final approval of the plan.

The review of data is important at this early point in the process, as the planning team must develop a firm understanding of "who we are" to eventually propose strategies for improvement. With data in hand, team members can spend some time in the first meeting reviewing and asking clarifying questions about the data and identifying other data they may want to consider. Before leaving, they should be tasked with studying the data on their own so they can come to the next meeting with a more complete understanding of the district's performance and characteristics.

If the district is developing a strategic plan to take the place of a recently expired plan, some of the data to be reviewed should include the school's current mission statement, core values, and other plan components that remain in place until a new plan is created (vision statement, portrait of a graduate, etc.). While there may be some tweaks to these components as the planning progresses, school leaders must be comfortable knowing that a strong mission statement may endure well beyond the five-year term for which it was adopted. In some districts, the mission has not changed

Table 13.1 Sample Agenda: Planning Team Meeting 1

- Introductions and ice-breaker
- Receive charge from School Board
- Review proposed timeline and process
- Begin review of data—including most recent plan, mission, and core values
- Assignment:
    - Identify and share sample plans
    - Continue individual review of data

in decades, and that's alright, so long as the decision to continue with the mission as it was stated fifteen or twenty years ago is one that is made collaboratively and thoughtfully.

Another important activity during the launch phase will be the opportunity to share sample plans from other schools. As mentioned in the pre-planning phase, you should have set up a digital folder into which each member of the team may post links to plans they have discovered that have one or more desirable components for consideration. While it is recognized that each school has its unique characteristics and challenges, reviewing plans from other districts can be an inspirational process, as team members identify components they would like to see included in the new plan.

As the team prepares for the second meeting, one goal should be to forge agreement on the components to be included in the new plan, as well as the data to be shared in the document and in communications to the staff and community during the planning discussions. With engaged planning team members who do their homework from the first meeting (reviewing data and plans from other schools), you can enter Meeting 2 determined to define the components and data to be included in the plan. Table 13.2 presents a sample agenda for the second meeting, which also includes an initial discussion of the all-important Mission Statement and Core Values.

As mentioned in Chapter 4, the importance of a clearly stated, easily recalled mission statement cannot be overstated. Schools too often attempt to develop a mission statement that identifies every possible goal they may have for virtually every student. In doing so, they create a complicated, lengthy statement—sometimes paragraphs or pages long that nobody remembers and few understand. Such statements are quickly disregarded and left to gather dust on the shelves in the district offices.

Table 13.2 Sample Agenda: Planning Team Meeting II

- Share thoughts of plan review from other schools
- Discuss preferred components and data to be shared in the plan
- Begin review of Mission and Core Beliefs
- Adopt plan for Community Foruml

On the other hand, a simple, one-sentence statement that can be easily reduced to a four- or five-word slogan (or less) is something almost everyone can remember and understand. A few examples include:

- *Empowering all students to lead fulfilling lives in a changing world ("Empowering all students")*
- *Providing a high-quality and equitable education supporting each student's academic, social, and emotional development ("Supporting each child")*
- *Developing a community of learners who are curious, resourceful, and respectful ("Developing resourceful learners")*

Begin by reviewing your existing mission statement and/or those of other schools and identify the phrases and terms that best describe who you want to be. Your mission should make a bold, yet reasonable declaration of what the school attempts to do on a day-to-day, year-to-year basis. The mission should be something to which all curriculum, programs, and activities can be tethered and drive decision-making throughout the district.

You should not expect to leave this second meeting with a mission statement finalized by the planning team, as you will be considering feedback from the staff and community through survey responses and public forums. However, you should lay the groundwork for the adoption of a concise, memorable, and meaningful statement by helping the team understand the importance of adopting a mission that serves to define what you want to accomplish as a school or district.

Similarly, at this second meeting, you are encouraged to begin identifying and defining those core values that are held in high regard throughout the district. Once again, a review of your existing core values and those expressed in plans from other districts can be a helpful strategy for defining those that are most important to the schools.

As with the mission statement, it can become quite easy to develop a list of core values that is lengthy and all-inclusive. Many experienced planners will encourage you to limit your list to somewhere between four and eight core values. If you try to adopt an exhaustive list, you risk reducing the impact of each value, as well as the ability for community members to remember and delineate them one from another.

To make the core values memorable, some schools attempt to create acronyms that line up with the school's mascot or a motivational term like

"RESPECT" or "PRIDE"—all of which is well and good if the letters being used provide words that actually align with core values that are meaningful and applicable. I would encourage you to agree upon the most accurate list of core values, first, and not worry about whether they provide you with a memorable acronym. If you choose well and keep the number manageable, you will end up with a set of core values that can be widely displayed, creating a common understanding of what the district values.

Phase 3: Assess

At this point, while you have looked at a significant amount of data, reviewed your existing strategic plan, and researched plans from other schools, you have not yet heard from the staff and community regarding their perspectives of the district. It is now time to turn to them and collect their insights about the school's strengths and challenges through three different structures:

- Staff feedback loops
- Community forums
- Community-wide surveys

Staff Feedback Loops

The staff feedback loop is an opportunity for school leadership to engage directly with staff at each of the district's schools and hear their celebrations and concerns. This is an excellent chance for leadership to model effective facilitation skills and to develop collegiality with employees at all levels of the organization. If the size of your district permits, the superintendent can engage directly in this work as the facilitator of the feedback. In larger districts, it may make more sense for this to be done by district-level directors who are viewed by the staff as direct conduits to the superintendent.

Regardless of who facilitates these meetings, authenticity and sincerity are critical. Feedback from the staff must be accepted as a high priority as you identify topics of importance to the schools. Inviting their input, collating their suggestions, and reporting back to them in the days following each feedback loop are critical to building trust, showing that they were heard and that their ideas have been documented for consideration by the planning team.

There are many formats for receiving input from staff in an hour-long meeting. We won't describe each of them here, but you are encouraged to explore various group facilitation strategies on your own and select one that feels right for your setting. Some that you may want to consider include:

- SWOT Analysis (Strengths, Weaknesses, Opportunities, and Threats)
- Affinity Mapping and Dot Voting
- World Café or Rotating Conversations
- Think-Pair-Share
- Nominal Group Technique
- 1-2-4 all

At the conclusion of each staff meeting, school leadership should collate and organize what was discussed, preparing a summary for the planning team, while also sharing it back with the staff. This will demonstrate transparency as you communicate concerns that were raised, even if those concerns do not present the school or its leadership in the most flattering light.

Public Forum

At around the same time as you are holding staff feedback loops, you will want to hold your first public forum and conduct a community-wide survey.

The public forum is an event that requires thoughtful planning. This is another opportunity for school leadership to demonstrate its willingness to engage with the wider public to hear their concerns and hopes for the schools, which is not always a pleasant experience. A well-organized forum goes a long way toward helping disenchanted community members feel they have been heard, while also encouraging those with positive outlooks to share their celebrations and aspirations for the schools.

Because the number of public forums is likely to be limited to just one or two evenings, this is a fantastic opportunity for the superintendent to serve as the face of the district. A superintendent who demonstrates the skills of an expert facilitator can foster a tremendous amount of trust with a large number of people at each forum. Turning facilitation over to an outside consultant or another leader in the district may be preferable for some. Even if that is the case, the superintendent should serve as the host for the meeting, demonstrating endorsement of the idea that community input is vital to the planning process.

Table 13.3 Sample Agenda: Public Forum 3—Part A

6:30-6:40 Welcome and overview of the evening
6:40-6:50 Who We Are - *Share a sampling of the data collected in the planning process.*
6:50-7:00 Overview of the Strategic Planning Process
7:00-7:10 Education today: Education tomorrow: *Show a video or present information that challenges us to think about what education should look like as we move into the second quarter of the 21st century.*

As with all meetings at which efficiency and effectiveness are important, the public forum should be scheduled with a hard stop time of no more than two hours. In that time, you can accomplish a great deal, following the sample agenda presented in Tables 13.3 and 13.4.

Table 13.4 Sample Agenda: Public Forum 3—Part B

7:10-7:15 Organize into Discussion Groups - *Each participant's name tag will indicate the table at which they are asked to participate.*

7:15-8:10 Facilitated Small Group Discussions - *Suggested prompt:*
As you reflect on the video and consider the data that has been shared, think about our schools and students in the context of current and future learning needs, and the challenges we face in helping our students meet those needs.
 	
1. When you examine our schools:
  o What do they do particularly well that they need to keep doing and use as a foundation for the future?
  o On the other hand, what areas require improvement and focused energy and resources?
  o What should the schools stop doing since it is not working?
 	
2. To help us develop our "Profile of a Graduate", what are the key characteristics/skills you believe each graduate should have to be ready for college, career, and citizenship?
 	
3. What innovative approaches to educating and operating might our schools consider to better prepare our students for the challenges ahead?
 	
4. How can our schools ensure high-quality learning for every student while remaining financially responsible and efficient? (How can the district focus its resources to maximize the opportunities we provide to our students?)

8:10-8:20   Sharing out of Discussion Highlights
8:20-8:30   Next Steps and Adjournment

Table 13.3 provides the agenda for the first half of the meeting, which is the presentation portion. Here, you will share data about the district, explain the planning process and timeline, and—if desired—share a video or data providing an overview of where education should be headed in order to best meet student needs in the coming decades.

In Table 13.4, the agenda continues with the public input portion of the meeting. This is where you will invite conversations at each table in response to prompts determined by the planning team. Suggested prompts are provided here merely to assist you in developing your own engaging ideas.

Holding a successful public forum can be tricky. You want to provide ample opportunity for input, yet you don't want the evening to drag on for several hours. You want to hear from as many people as possible without allowing one or two individuals to dominate the airwaves, and you want to provide data that accurately depicts the school's current characteristics and performance without depleting time for others to share their perspectives.

To do it well, you must plan not only the vision you have for the meeting but also the nuts and bolts of the evening's mechanics. Table 13.5 provides some helpful suggestions for organizing and balancing your forum for maximum effectiveness.

Following the forum, identify two or three members of the planning team who will collate the feedback received and organize it into themes that emerged throughout the evening. For example, if it was mentioned at several tables that hiring and retaining top-notch teachers is an important challenge for the school, you may want to create a category entitled "Highly Skilled Educators," and group any comments pertaining to the professional staff under that heading.

These themes will be used later in the planning process, but they are not written in stone. These are simply the major themes identified by this small group as they reviewed input from the forum. When this information is shared with the full planning team, the categories may change, but it is important to start with something for the full team to respond to.

While it would be preferable to end up with no more than four to six major themes identified for your strategic planning purposes, it is likely you may have eight to ten themes (or even more) at this stage in the process. Once you take the next step, which involves conducting a community-wide

Table 13.5 Tips for a Successful Public Forum

1. Organize the room into tables at which 6–10 participants may sit comfortably and hear one another without being interrupted by noise from other tables. A large cafeteria with round tables works well.

2. Set up a sign-in table, where participants pick up a nametag and are randomly assigned a table number at which to sit for the discussion portion of the evening. This can be done by placing a table number on the nametag for each person. Think about splitting up people who arrive together, so their perspectives are heard at different tables.

3. Prepare members of the leadership team, School Board, and/or planning team to serve as facilitators at each table, so you have leadership representation distributed throughout the room, rather than having them miss out on this chance to hear directly from community members.

4. Use a space with one or more large screens to which you can project the agenda and any videos or data slides you will be sharing.

5. Select the data you wish to share and organize it into attractive, easily understood charts, graphs, and tables.

6. Identify a short (5-minute) media clip you would like to share that addresses one or more topics of importance to the community or education in general. This is shared early in the evening to promote reflection and set the stage for innovative thinking.

7. Set up your entire agenda on one slide deck, with a handout or takeaway document summarizing the evening's activities.

8. Have each table assign a notetaker/reporter (can be two different people) who will share with the larger group common themes that came out during the table discussions.

9. Determine who will serve as a timekeeper – this individual will keep the evening moving according to schedule.

10. Look through each item on the agenda and assign a facilitator to each. Recognize that a strong presentation of data, efficient facilitation of the discussion groups, a clear description of how the feedback will be used, and what the next steps will be in the planning process are key characteristics of a successful public forum.

survey, you will have a more focused picture of what is important to the staff, families, and community members.

Community-Wide Survey

The digital and social media age has made it very easy to collect and collate a large amount of data in a relatively short amount of time. Community surveys can now be created using a variety of web-based options, each with the capability to disaggregate the data and provide you with useful information that allows for the identification of trends and themes that might otherwise have gone unnoticed. Selecting the best platform for your district involves understanding which software licenses you currently own and what their capabilities are.

While assessing the various options, be sure your license provides you with the capacity to receive responses from the number of participants you hope to survey. You will also want to use an instrument that demonstrates flexibility in how the questions may be structured (multiple choice, drop-down, Likert scale, open-ended, etc.) and one that can disaggregate data according to the roles each respondent plays in the district (parent, teacher, support staff, student, etc.).

One of the common errors in conducting a survey of this magnitude is attempting to ask every possible question you can think of. This is the same trap that some fall into when they write a mission statement that attempts to cover every possible situation that may arise throughout the school year; it's just too much and unnecessary. Keep your survey short; ten questions or fewer are fine. Craft it in a way that allows you to determine what your constituents want to see improved, along with what they think is going well.

Table 13.6 provides a sample survey that has been adapted in one form or another by more than a handful of schools looking to gather input from a large number of community members.

Whatever questions you decide to ask in your survey, be sure the options for answers are comprehensive and clear to the participants. If you allow bias to enter into the construction of the survey by limiting responses only to those items with which you are in favor, you will limit the accuracy with which the responses reflect the community's wishes. Even if there are answers you are not excited to receive, they must be included so you can determine if your vision for the schools aligns with that of the community. If it doesn't, you will at least have a fair warning of the disconnect.

The survey should be distributed to all families and staff in the district. You may also want to consider sending it to high school students—and possibly upper middle school students, though it may look a little different for younger students than for community members. Specific invitations to participate should be provided to community leaders and elected officials, while the

Table 13.6 Sample Strategic Planning Survey

Our schools have begun a strategic planning process to define the decisions and actions that will guide the direction of our district over the next several years.

One of the most important components of this effort is community input. We will begin collecting input through this short survey and will provide additional opportunities throughout this school year for further engagement in the process.

All survey responses are anonymous.
Thank you for lending your voice to education in our community.

1. Please check each of the following statements that describe you:
   Business Owner
   Civic or government leader
   Elected official
   Graduate
   Parent/guardian of current students
   Not a parent/guardian of current students
   Parent/guardian of graduates
   Senior citizen
   Student
   Support personnel
   Teacher or administrator
   Other (please specify)

2. What do you feel most proud of when you think about our schools? (Please select up to four)
   Achievement of our students
   The academic program
   The athletic program
   The fine arts and performing arts programs
   The schools as a steward of taxpayer funds
   The promotion of opportunity and access for all students
   The school facilities
   The educational staff
   The schools' focus on positive relationships
   Community and family support and engagement
   Adherence to core values
   The district's focus on its mission
   How the schools help students lead fulfilling lives
   The level of individualization/personalization provided to students
   If you feel your choice was not represented for the question above, please list it here:

3. What do you think are the top four challenges facing students today? These may be Community, family, and/or socio-economic issues that are not necessarily the responsibility of the school district. (Please select up to four)
   A changing economy; fewer high-paying jobs
   Social media
   Stress and anxiety

Table 13.6 *Continued*

> Being ready for college or the workplace
> Drugs, alcohol, vaping
> Lack of support at school
> Lack of support at home
> Global competition
> Equity of opportunities and access
> Establishing positive peer relationships
> Rapidly changing world
> Socio-emotional challenges
> Stigmas around certain pathways
> Personal financial concerns
> Artificial Intelligence
> If you feel your choice was not represented for the question above, please list it here:
>
> 4. What do you believe should be the top areas of focus for our schools to provide for our students? (Please select up to four)
>   Providing highly qualified staff/teachers
>   Implementing rigorous, challenging programs
>   Ensuring meaningful socio-emotional learning
>   Producing high standardized test scores
>   Achieving high college admission and matriculation rates
>   Ensuring equitable access to programming for all students
>   Providing safe, engaging, and healthy extracurricular programs
>   Offering extensive Career and Technical Education (CTE)
>   Providing alternative learning programs
>   Ensuring a safe, nurturing, and well-managed learning environment
>   Hiring and maintaining a staff that is diverse in characteristics and experiences
>   Ensuring diverse voices and perspective are represented in the curriculum
>   Developing students who are good citizens
>   If you feel your choice was not represented for the question above, please list it here:
>
> 5. What do you think are the top three challenges faced by our schools? (Please select up to three)
>   Providing challenging instructional programs
>   Recruiting and retaining highly qualified staff
>   Expanding communication and community involvement
>   School funding issues
>   Increasing student achievement
>   Providing access and opportunities for all students
>   Supporting students with varied needs
>   Providing a safe, orderly environment
>   Keeping pace with enrollment growth
>   If you feel your choice was not represented for the question above, please list it here:

(Continued)

Table 13.6 *Continued*

6. Which of the following would be the most important to add or expand in school programming? (Please select up to three) Early childhood (Pre-kindergarten) Elementary world languages Science, Technology, Engineering, Arts and Mathematics (STEAM) at elementary level Alternative pathways to graduation Career education Financial literacy Elementary health education Experiential learning If you feel your choice was not represented for the question above, please list it here:
7. Which of the following deserves our greatest attention for improvement or expansion? (Please select up to three) Science Technology Engineering and Maker programming Mathematics Computer science Career and technical (vocational) education Language arts Social studies Visual arts Performing arts Health, wellness and physical education World languages Library-media programming School counseling Social work services Instructional support Student health services Socio-emotional learning Extra-curricular programs
8. Please identify other ideas you would like to share that would help the Strategic planning team as they develop a five-year plan to direct the future of our schools.

link may also be posted to community webpages or distributed through organizations like the City Clerk's office, the local Chamber of Commerce, and other groups with a broad reach in the community.

Two weeks is ample time during which to receive a large number of responses to the survey. When you send the survey link out to all families and staff with an explanatory cover letter, you'll likely receive a flurry of responses within the first forty-eight hours, followed by a quiet period of three to five days. A reminder email after the first week will create a second spike in activity and a final reminder the day before the survey closes will produce a third and final rush that will provide you with a solid number of respondents.

With the survey data in hand, you will want someone with a firm grasp of survey technology to assist with the presentation of data. While it is fine to share the raw data with the entire planning team, it is advisable to present some of the data in disaggregated form. Team members will want to know, "What did the teachers say is the biggest challenge?" "What is it that parents want from our schools?" "What do the students feel is missing from our programming?"

Once the staff feedback, public forum, and survey data are collated, disaggregated, and organized, you have what you need to complete the final task in the assessment phase, which is identifying the strengths, weaknesses, and hopes for your school programming (according to your constituents). The organization of this data will provide you with the framework for your strategic plan, which you will attempt to develop during your third planning team meeting.

As illustrated in Table 13.7, there are several critical aspects to this meeting. One major goal of this meeting is to develop a first draft of the organization's mission statement and core beliefs. If you are working from an existing statement, this is an easier goal to meet, but if you are creating an entirely new document, the review of other plans and the feedback received from the faculty and community will be critical in driving this discussion.

Table 13.7 Sample Agenda: Planning Team Meeting III

- Revisit Mission and Core Beliefs—with a goal of developing draft 1
- Review input from Survey, Community Forum, and Staff Feedback Loop
- Identify proposed focus areas (themes)
- Assign a subgroup for each Focus Area
    - Create vision statement and rationale for the Focus Area
    - Create three to five goals for the Focus Area

As you decide upon your draft statements, keep these important principles in mind:

- Keep the mission short, aspirational, and memorable. One sentence that can be reduced to a meaningful slogan is all that is needed to drive the work.
- Keep the number of core beliefs between four and eight. Selecting any more than that makes them difficult to remember.

Phase 4: Goal-Setting

The other major goal of this meeting is to identify the overarching focus areas into which the team will eventually divide the action strategies of the plan. These focus areas—also known as planks or themes—provide an organizational framework for the school's targeted efforts. Typically, schools are able to separate their goals and action items under headings related to students, staff, families, community, programming, and resources, with more specific headers that provide further definitions within each area. For example, a school may determine that they want to title one focus area "Highly engaged students" and another "Well-managed resources."

It is clearly a team decision how to identify the focus areas within the plan, and those names may evolve during the planning process. The final steps to be taken during this meeting are to ask members to divide themselves evenly into subgroups representing each of the identified focus areas and to assign each group its homework. Leaving this third meeting with a draft of the focus areas provides everyone on the team with a clearer understanding of where they are headed, and the planning process begins to seem less daunting.

Dividing into subgroups can usually be done voluntarily, though it is not uncommon for one or more areas to appeal to a larger number of participants. Pointing out that being placed on one of the subgroups does not mean members will not have input or work on the other focus areas, as the planning process will provide for those opportunities, but this is just a starting point that will provide each area the collaborative effort necessary to move the process along.

Once the subgroups are identified, they should be tasked with (1) creating a vision statement for their focus area, (2) identifying the rationale behind the vision statement, and (3) creating three to five proposed goals for their area. This will require each subgroup to work together prior to the next planning team meeting.

The vision statement for each area can be thought of as the statement that provides a further definition as to what it is that the school hopes to provide or accomplish in this area, while the rationale identifies why this is an area of importance. For example, a district may structure one area as follows:

Focus Area 1: Highly Skilled Educators

Vision Statement: Our schools will be filled with adults who place the needs of students first, who engage in ongoing, meaningful professional development to ensure expert care and instruction are being provided in every setting to every student, and who feel valued by our community through appropriate and competitive compensation, recognition, and empowerment.

Rationale: Highly skilled, well-supported staff provide students with meaningful instruction and care, promoting lifelong learning and the development of healthy relationships that lead to fulfilling lives.
Goals:

1. Attract, hire, and retain highly qualified, student-centered teachers and support personnel who represent the diversity of our students and community at all levels of the organization.
2. Provide meaningful professional development and supervision that supports the school's goals, promotes innovation, and empowers teachers to continually improve curriculum and instruction.
3. Provide a positive work environment in which teachers and support personnel are valued and have a voice in matters of importance to them.

While the final product may look very different, this seminal work by each subgroup begins to form a frame on which the team will create its overall plan. Working in small groups is much more efficient during this writing stage, and each team member will have the opportunity to review and offer edits to each of the focus areas in the coming weeks.

Phase 5: Planning

The next few months of the planning process are the most gratifying for those who are eager to see a plan come together. This is when the team will draft, revise, and refine each of the components of the plan. Rather than suggest agendas for the next few meetings, it is assumed that at this stage, the team has likely started to determine the mechanisms and format that work best for them, so those agendas can be developed locally. Thoughtful development of each agenda will keep the momentum going, and a few suggestions are offered here to keep each member engaged in the process.

First, it is important to find ways to give each member the opportunity to work on focus areas other than the one for which they were originally selected. This is critical for several reasons:

- Allows for a variety of perspectives to be shared in each Area
- Provides each member with a feeling of ownership in the overall plan, thereby increasing buy-in
- Removes the danger that comes when a person only works on one Focus Area and develops an unhealthy sense of authorship and defensiveness about that Area

Mixing up the subgroups during the planning phase is easily done. After the initial development of Focus Area statements (vision, rationale, goals), simply reassign members to other teams (voluntarily, if possible). This gives each member new subgroup teammates with whom to work and a new Focus Area on which to work while accomplishing the goal of increasing the perspectives being lent to each area.

A second suggestion at this point is to seek agreement on the mission and core values early in the planning phase. By the fourth meeting, the team should have reached a consensus on these two important components of the plan. However, it is recommended that you include these items at the top of each agenda for two reasons:

- Since your plan should be anchored by these two components—and possibly a vision statement—it is good to keep these at the forefront of your work.

- During the planning process, the discussions you have may cause you to rethink a phrase in the mission statement, or to reconsider one or more of the core values. It's ok to go back and make edits—nothing is in stone at this point.

Finally, for the planning phase to move forward efficiently and be completed in a timely fashion, the school's leadership team will need to be focused on reviewing, editing, and formatting the work being done by the planning team. Leaving this work for planning team meetings will bog down the process and delay completion considerably.

After each meeting, one or more members of the leadership team should collate the work completed and serve as the repository for any work done by subgroups between meetings. This allows for the document to evolve more efficiently toward its final format, ensures a single source for the most updated version of the plan, and provides a standardized writing style for the entire plan.

Performance Measures

As the plan comes together, with the Mission/Vision/Core Values adopted, focus areas with rationale and goal statements finalized, the team can identify the performance measures that will be used to determine the school's success. These should be aspirational but realistic. For example, while it is certainly a laudable goal that 100 percent of your students are reading at grade level by Grade 3, you may be working in a community in which that number has hovered around 65 percent for the past decade or more. In that case, it may be more reasonable to set a goal of 85 percent by the fifth year of the plan, increasing by 4 percent each year.

Because of their expertise, the educational leaders on the planning team should be encouraged to develop a proposed set of performance indicators toward which the school will work. While these will most likely be amended by the planning team, presenting a list that has been developed by the school's leadership is a good way to start the conversation from an informed standpoint, rather than working from scratch in a team meeting.

Search for data points that move your school away from standardized test scores on statewide assessments. These are often the least reliable measures of where our students are and how well they are doing. Especially at the high school level, where some students may put very little effort into taking an assessment that has no bearing on their transcript or college application, these assessments provide schools with little information that is helpful. Local assessments, or assessments that are nationally normed and individually adjusted, often provide you with your best measures of academic growth and performance. A potential list of performance indicators may include data points mentioned earlier in Chapter 12 (Figure 12.3).

The next step in the planning phase is to determine how the team will gather input on what they have developed, which is done most effectively through a second round of faculty feedback loops and a second community forum in the next phase of the process.

Phase 6: Present and Refine

During this round of input, the planning team should share some of the data that was compiled after the first round of input (survey responses, SWOT analysis, etc.) as well as an overview of their work thus far. This may be done at a public forum and through staff meetings where feedback is sought on the team's work to date. While it is not necessary to share the complete draft of what has been created at this point, it is important to present the mission/vision statements, the core values, and the overarching focus areas.

When identifying the focus areas, it may be helpful to give examples of the types of goals that could be set in each, but it is not critical that you delve too far into the individual rationale statements and objectives, as a large group can get sidetracked with wordsmithing too easily. It is better to keep the presentation at a high level at this point and seek feedback on the development of the mission and vision, along with the core values. If you get those things right, you will provide the school with a solid foundation on which to make ongoing improvements, and the rest of the plan becomes a guidebook for the next few years.

Similar to the first round of input, an organized structure for both the faculty feedback loop and the public forum will allow the team to gather the data they need to ensure the work they are doing is aligned with the community's hopes for the school. Structure the meetings with a brief presentation of the data and work to date, followed by small group discussions in which participants share their reactions to the drafts of the mission/vision/core values/focus areas. Ask questions such as:

- Does the mission statement align with what we hope to be doing in our schools on a daily and yearly basis?
- Do the core values reflect on who we are—and who we hope to be—as a community?
- Are there any glaring omissions?

Once you receive input from faculty and the community, the planning team can get back to work refining the plan—making edits where necessary and finalizing each component of the plan based on the feedback received. This will require several (three to four, typically) meetings of the planning team—and possibly one or two meetings of subgroups, as well.

Throughout the refinement phase, members of the district leadership team should identify data and resources that may be presented and indexed in the plan. While the plan is a look ahead to the next three, five, or ten years, it is important to present the data that illustrates the school's current characteristics and performance. This will set the stage for the focus areas and objectives that will be presented later in the plan. Consider including demographic, performance, and organizational data that will provide a clear picture of "who we are" without overwhelming the reader. Presented in easy-to-understand charts, tables, and graphs, this data will present the baseline from which the school will work moving forward.

The refinement phase can become laborious if members are allowed to hijack discussions by wordsmithing or arguing minute points. It takes a skilled and deliberate facilitator to keep the conversation moving without stifling meaningful dialogue. At some moments the facilitator will need to ask the group for its consensus on a particular item in order to bring closure to the discussion, helping members understand that minor wording changes throughout the document (other than the mission and core values) should not be cause for lengthy deliberations. If the group can keep its focus on ensuring clear intent within each focus area, the plan will be effective at driving positive change.

For Thought or Discussion
1. How will you engage staff in developing your strategic plan? Start thinking now about how you will structure the first round of faculty input so you may have meaningful and efficient staff meetings. Remember, less is more in terms of the meeting itself, so develop one or two activities that will keep them engaged and provide you with the information you need regarding their concerns and hopes.
2. Now is a good time to begin planning the public forum as well. Develop a presentation that gives a quick overview of district data and the planning process—no more than fifteen minutes or so in length, which will allow for some questions.
3. Take a look at the sample survey provided in this Figure 13.6. Will this survey meet your needs, or are there other questions you will want to ask?
4. Do you have an existing mission statement? Core values? If not, are there examples out there that you might use to inspire thinking on your planning team? Be prepared to share these at the outset in order to get the process moving in a positive direction.
5. Once you have survey data and feedback from faculty and the community, spend some time thinking about the focus areas you might propose for your plan. Discuss these with your leadership team.

14 Strategic Planning
Putting the Plan to Work

Once the refining stage of your strategic planning process is completed, you will have a complete draft of your plan. Congratulations! It is now time to present the draft to the School Board for final review and adoption.

Phase 7: Approve and Disseminate

If you are successful in developing a clearly stated charge for the Planning Team, your remaining work will be much easier than the work of the past several months. This is a good time to remind the planning team that the Board has the authority to edit and approve the document and determine how you will present the draft at an upcoming Board meeting. Having several, if not all, members of the planning team attend the Board presentation is an impressive show of unity and provides the Board with the opportunity to recognize each member for their work over the past year.

The plan should be in a format that can be adopted as presented by the Board. More than likely, there will be some suggested edits to both content and format, and you should be prepared to discuss and, if necessary, make those adjustments as directed by the Board. Again, keep in mind that the most important pieces to the plan are the mission, vision, and core values. Don't get caught up arguing semantics in other parts of the plan, as those arguments will likely not impact the work to be done in the long run. As long as the plan identifies the areas to be focused on and the objectives to be gained, the school will have a document that works.

A formal vote by the School Board signifies the completion of the plan and a commitment to the statements, values, and objectives identified therein. It will likely take two meetings to get to this point, as the Board will want time to review and discuss this critical document. Setting up a two-step approval process, with a first and second reading at two successive Board meetings, provides the public with an additional opportunity to share thoughts about the plan.

Although it has been important for the school leadership to be very visible and engaged throughout the planning process, consider allowing other members of the Planning Team to present the proposed draft to the School Board. This sends the message that the document is the result of a collaborative effort of the larger community and not just the work of the superintendent.

As part of the presentation, it is important to review the planning process that has been followed to date, indicating the number of participants who were present at each faculty meeting and public forum, as well as the number of respondents who provided input through the community survey. This provides the School Board with a clearer understanding of the Team's engagement with a wide range of constituents, further justifying the Team's decisions.

Presenting the draft plan through a professionally formatted digital and hard-copy presentation gives the Board confidence that a great deal of thought has been put into the proposal. Your presenters should spend a few minutes explaining the various components of the plan, emphasizing the development of the mission statement and core values. These will be the main drivers of decision-making in the district for as long as this plan is in place, and it is important that the Board understands their significance.

Once the plan is approved by the Board, the focus turns to the internal work of the district leadership. Whether the school has talented digital content experts in-house or hires an outside firm, the final layout of the plan should provide an attractive, easy-to-follow format that is adaptable to both print and digital platforms.

Posting the plan to the school website and promoting the mission statement or slogan at the head of every page is a critical first step in ensuring the message is delivered to all who visit the site. This is not the only way to promote the mission of the school, but it is one easy way to state clearly and consistently what the school is about.

If you have set up a webpage to share the planning team's progress, you can now transition that page into one that presents the proposed plan in its entirety. Be sure Strategic Planning is one of the directory headings on the main page of your website—the plan should be no more than two clicks away from your landing page, making it easily accessible by anyone interested in your work.

As soon as the webpage is up and running, announce the adoption of the plan and provide the link to all members of the staff, all families, and throughout the wider community. This is an exciting step in the school's growth and one that should be publicized to the greatest extent possible.

Printed copies of the plan should be made for every member of the staff—along with enough copies to cover new hires who are brought on board during the duration of the plan. Having dozens—or hundreds—of extra hard copies at each school will also allow for wider dissemination. Print copies are nice to have because of their usability when holding faculty discussions addressing the work to be done. Teachers and administrators with a copy of the plan on their desks can easily access the information, share it with students and others, and ensure the plan remains at the forefront of their work with one another.

Consider distributing the hard copies at the first staff meeting after adoption as a way to mark the completion of the project as well as the embarkation of the work to be done. This should be celebratory and affirming for the staff, as well as an indicator of the opportunities and challenges ahead. Staff will want to know this is not a document that is going to sit on a shelf, but one that will drive their work in the coming years. The unveiling and distribution of the plan should be seen as a chance to unify the staff around a central mission and set of core values, creating a common understanding of what the school stands for and where it is headed.

Phase 8: Operationalizing

While the development and consistent implementation of a strategic plan is one of the most effective steps an organization can take to build trust among all constituents, the development of a plan that disappears shortly after adoption, only to sit on a shelf and collect dust until the next planning cycle comes around, is one of the surest ways to degrade trust over an extended period of time. One can imagine the cynicism that is fostered when staff realize the plan has not been referred to in several years—especially after the focus it was given during the planning phase. Unfortunately, this is too often the case, and the day-to-day challenges of running the school take precedence over the implementation of the plan.

When this happens, the breakdown in trust is just one casualty for the school. Lack of focus, duplication of effort, conflict, and confusion are additional outgrowths of the lack of a coordinated effort with established goals, performance indicators, and responsibilities. After all the effort to put a plan in place, it is critical that school leaders take the last two steps in the process—the first of which is to operationalize the plan by identifying who will do what, by when, and how completion will be demonstrated.

To operationalize the plan is to develop a roadmap for completing the action items identified. This can be done in any number of ways—the simplest of which may be to collaboratively develop an operations matrix (Table 14.1) that identifies the timeline, responsible party, and specific steps to be taken to address each strategy identified in the plan.

As shown here, the leadership team can operationalize the plan by addressing each strategy identified in the document, clarifying the action steps that will be taken at each school, the year in which the steps will be taken, who will take the lead, and how progress will be demonstrated. Planning at this granular level ensures the 20,000-foot view provided in the planning document is condensed into manageable steps that make a difference for students.

Phase 9: Promotion and Implementation

There are a multitude of ways to ensure your Strategic Plan is a living document that drives the work in your district. It is critical that sharing and promotion of the plan begin with the superintendent and are supported by building and district leaders in their interactions with staff, students, and families. Without this enthusiasm, there will be no buy-in from constituents, and you will risk having a plan that eventually fades from memory, leaving you with a muddled approach to progress.

As mentioned in Chapter 4, it is critical to start this process at the very beginning of each school year—during the onboarding of new staff and the

Table 14.1 Operations Matrix

Strategy	Action steps	Targeted year of completion	Primary Responsibility	Progress indicators
Leverage daily Morning Meetings and Advisory Groups to build positive relationships between and among students and staff.	Elementary Schools Focus professional development (PD) on Responsive Classroom (RC) for the 2024-25 school year. All staff will engage in RC learning opportunities led by our consultant that will enhance a school-wide approach to Morning Meeting. Middle School Review the Advisory structure, including a review of the purpose of the program and adjust to best meet student needs. High School Design Social-Emotional Learning activities that address age- and developmentally appropriate needs, allow for equitable access and align with our Core Values.	1	Prek-12 Building Administrators	*Elementary Schools* Morning meetings will be built into the schedule each day. Responsive Classroom training will be completed by all teachers during the first three days of school, with follow-up training in October. *Middle School* Staff will engage in data collection and discussions regarding Advisory effectiveness during PD time in September. Proposed changes will follow the collaborative decision-making model, with implementation by December. *High School* Student Support Team will propose activities appropriate for each grade-level advisory. At least one new activity will be implemented each month.

Strategic Planning: Putting the Plan to Work 197

welcoming back of veteran staff in the fall. This is an excellent opportunity to introduce your colleagues to the district plan—focusing largely on mission and core values.

Although the plan itself may present a wide range of action strategies and performance measures, it is not necessary to go into great detail at this point. It is most important that your staff understand the district's commitment to the mission and core values; hearing it directly from school leaders on their first day at work goes a long way toward creating the culture you want for your schools.

School Improvement Plans

Once the leadership team has operationalized the Strategic Plan and identified action strategies to be employed each year, schools throughout the district can easily develop annual improvement plans that address the identified strategies. For example, referring to Table 14.1, the High School's Student Support Team has been tasked with researching and proposing activities appropriate for each grade-level advisory during the first year of the plan's implementation. This provides the High School leadership with a very tangible step to be taken that is directly tied to the Strategic Plan.

The operational matrix goes on to say, "At least one new activity will be implemented each month, from September through May." This provides the school with another easily measurable goal and an activity that will have an immediate impact on students. This is where the rubber hits the road when it comes to strategic planning. Rather than simply crafting a high-level view of where the school should be headed, operationalizing the plan provides specific steps that become part of each school's annual improvement plan.

Leadership Goals

Because schools should measure what is important, a Strategic Plan is made even more viable when school leaders craft their annual professional goals to align with it. Continuing the example from above, the High School principal in this scenario would be encouraged to create goals tied to improvements made in the school's advisory program. This brings the plan all the way down from that visionary 20,000-foot view and into the classroom, which is the only way the plan remains relevant.

To further emphasize the school's commitment to the plan, school leaders' goals should be tied directly to their annual evaluation, with mid-year check-ins to encourage adequate progress. When we do this, we are not only setting lofty goals for the year, but we are also revisiting those goals and measuring our performance against those goals throughout the year. If your evaluation process is robust and meaningful, progress toward accomplishing the strategies identified in the Strategic Plan will be steady and persistent.

When each school's improvement plan and leadership goals are tied directly to the Strategic Plan, the district will experience cohesiveness and singularity of purpose at a higher level. Staff throughout the district will be aware of the plan and its importance to the community, and they will speak with more consistency about the mission and core values shared by all schools.

School Board Priorities

Another significant way to emphasize the importance of the Strategic Plan is to ensure the School Board develops annual priorities and goals that reflect the Focus Areas identified in the plan. These priorities should be discussed and voted upon at a public meeting near the start of the school year and publicized through regular Board communication channels (newsletters, website, etc.).

The following is an example of School Board priorities and goals for one year:

School Board Priority 1: Safe and Equitable School Culture and Climate

a   Continue to support the work of district staff in ensuring authentic practices and policies are in place to provide high-quality academic, personal wellness, and extracurricular programming with equity of access for all students.

b   Work with the District Leadership Team to promote and further accessibility of existing programs and ensure equitable access for all students.

c   Provide the resources and support necessary to address the response matrix of the Equity Audit, specifically around student safety and staff development.

By declaring its priorities and goals, the Board takes a significant and visible step in ensuring the Strategic Plan remains a living document that provides direction and purpose for the schools. In order for the Board's goals to be met, though, there must be administrative commitment to the goals. In the best-case scenario, the superintendent works with the Board to develop priorities and goals aligned with the Strategic Plan and the operational matrix.

Once the Board takes action, the superintendent should identify annual goals in alignment with the Board's priorities. Following the example above, the superintendent may adopt a goal as shown here:

Superintendent Goal 1: Ensuring a Safe and Equitable School Culture and Climate

a Oversee implementation of the School District's response to the Equity Review, providing an annual report to the School Board identifying tasks completed and those still in the planning stages.

b Support building-based administration in ensuring schools are safe places for all students, focusing on professional development regarding hateful symbols and language, studying the impact of electronic devices on the socio-emotional well-being of students (and leading a subsequent policy analysis), and engaging parents in better understanding of the impact of substance use and abuse.

As with school-based leaders, the superintendent's annual evaluation process—including mid-year reporting and check-ins—should be tied to the completion of the stated goals. In some districts, performance pay may be part of the evaluation process, with school leaders receiving a percentage of the potential annual payout determined by their ability to meet their school's or district's goals. This approach, long a hallmark of private sector corporations, has become more popular in PreK-12 schools in recent years. If a performance pay program is in place, the determination of payment should be tied to the attainment of goals as determined by the Strategic Plan.

Essentially, moving the Strategic Plan from a high-level, visionary document to one that drives decision-making and leads to specific actions at the classroom level requires intentional steps at all layers of the organization. A good way to view the flow of information is illustrated in Figure 14.1, where parallel pathways drive the work of the schools aligned to the plan.

As illustrated here, there are two paths by which the strategic plan is pushed forward. Along one path, the School Board sets its priorities and goals, which drive the goal-setting for the superintendent. The superintendent's evaluation, completed by the School Board each year, is then centered around the work defined in the Strategic Plan.

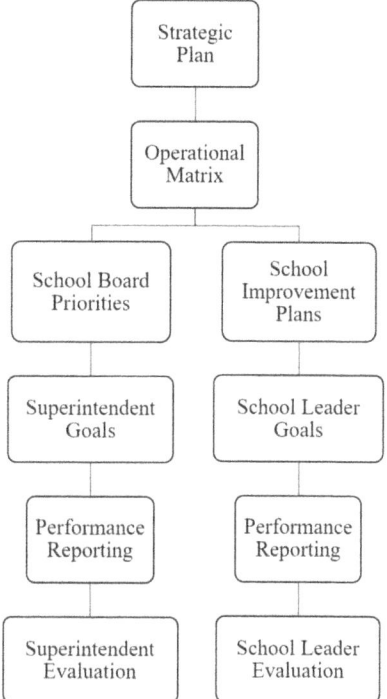

Figure 14.1. Strategic Plan Implementation.

Along the second, parallel path, the district's leadership team—under the direction of the superintendent—develops school-based plans to complete the work necessary to meet the goals in the Strategic Plan. Those leaders are then evaluated in part based on the work completed and the performance targets reached each year.

By adopting this approach, the district maintains a focus on the Strategic Plan at the Board, superintendent, and leadership levels. This focus encourages forward progress in a deliberate, coordinated manner and ensures that the plan remains a viable document throughout its intended implementation period.

Performance Measures and Reports

As noted above, the final step in the implementation of the Strategic Plan is to measure and report on the school's successes and challenges in meeting the targets identified in the Plan. This brings us full circle to Table 12.3 in Chapter 12, where we considered the potential data points to be considered in the planning process. Here at the implementation phase, schools report on the identified performance targets on an annual or semi-annual (twice-per-year) basis.

Sharing yearly progress through normal channels (Board meetings, newsletters, website, etc.), the administration demonstrates transparency and continued commitment to the Strategic Plan. This is critical to ensuring the plan's viability, and doing so builds trust with those who participated in the planning process, which could be most of the community, depending on how many participants you engaged through forums and surveys. Performance reporting keeps the plan at the center of your work with students and ensures consistency of effort—and commonality of purpose—throughout the school and over several years.

This final phase in Strategic Planning is too often overlooked as schools set the plan on the shelf and fall back into their comfortable routines. With focused effort, you can ensure that the plan coordinates the efforts you are making for students.

Operationalizing the plan, developing goals based on the plan, and evaluating our leaders' and students' progress against the standards defined in the plan ensure all of our work is not for naught. Through this intentional effort, we create a culture in which the entire school community knows—or can easily find—what we stand for, what our goals are, and how we're going about the work of meeting those goals.

For Thought and Discussion
1. How will you operationalize your plan? Who will be involved? Develop your schedule for creating the internal document that will drive your work over the course of this plan.
2. What actions must be taken each year in order to bring the plan to fruition? Who will be responsible for each action? Defining this clearly will help you keep the plan alive.

3. With your plan completed, take some time to identify all the places where it will be promoted. Digital media, print documents, etc.

4. How will you make sure this plan remains at the forefront of your work? Identify strategies for incorporating the plan in your leadership meetings/faculty meetings/opening of school/on-boarding, etc.

5. How will you ensure administrators' goals and school improvement plans are aligned to the strategic plan? Who will be responsible for developing the goals and plans at each school?

15 Leading with Intent

The importance of trust in any organization has been clearly established. In schools, where effectiveness and efficiency rely so heavily on the relationships that exist between educators, students, parents, and the community—and where the intended outcomes are measured not by units sold but by human performance—trusted leadership may be the most critical characteristic leading to organizational efficacy. Only when school leaders have fostered trust throughout all layers of the organization and with all constituent groups can they be sure that the school is operating most effectively.

While most school leaders recognize this fact, we too often log onto our favorite news sites each day and read stories about schools where trust has been shaken or shattered. When that occurs, not only are student experiences negatively impacted, but their very futures and the futures of students who will follow them are at stake. The outcomes are too important to be left to chance; school leaders must be intentional about their approach to every situation and to the long-term aspects of the work.

Throughout this book, you have been exposed to ideas and examples from experienced leaders who have implemented intentional strategies to nurture and maintain trust in their schools. None of the contributors—including myself—provided the examples as a way of declaring our perfection as school leaders. Each simply responded to the request to share practical examples of something that worked in their setting, so others may learn from their experiences. In reading these examples, you can reflect on how each strategy may work in your setting.

Being intentional about your approach is the first step toward leading a trust-filled school. It requires reflection about your own attitudes, principles, and goals, along with a focus on long-term planning that guides the school toward a shared mission driven by a set of core values. Without this combination of reflection and intentionality, the school is more likely to simply "get by" from one day and one year to the next.

While each of the ideas shared throughout this book may seem like a viable strategy for your school, I would caution against taking on all of them—or even a significant number of them—without a great deal of planning and deliberation. In order for the implementation of any of these ideas to result in the intended outcome for your school, each must fit into the larger scheme of your school's mission and—even better—your strategic plan.

You must begin there, with a collaboratively developed, meaningful understanding of who you are as a school leader, then work with your constituents to determine what you hope to provide for your students. With a well-crafted mission and defined core values in place, you can lead the school intentionally in the actions that will bring that mission to life. Ideas like those shared in previous chapters, adapted to meet the unique setting within your own school, can then be applied in a cohesive, thoughtful manner, with input from the necessary constituents in each situation.

Collaboration is key. The only strategies you should apply unilaterally are those that dictate your own behavior and approach to the work, such as your commitment to being an empowerment-centered leader, authentically visible, with a commitment to empathy. The larger strategies shared here—like making use of developing a strategic plan, implementing student-led IEPs, or forming a business-school roundtable, all require collaboration with colleagues, students, families, or the community, as defined by each setting.

Once you are committed to a trust-filled organization, spend some time reflecting on your own leadership. You may conduct a self-assessment, like that provided in Table 15.1, which was largely developed using Claude 3.7 Sonnet (2025) and modified for the purposes of this chapter.

To truly understand how your leadership impacts school culture, consider seeking input from others who work most closely with you. Teacher leaders, school board members, public officials, and leaders of parent groups and booster clubs can provide some insight into how your leadership is perceived by others. An anonymous survey provides them with a safe place to share their thoughts, which can be done as part of the annual evaluation process. You can simply modify the self-assessment questions for distribution to those constituents from whom you are seeking input, as shown in Table 15.2.

Table 15.1 School Leader Self-Assessment

For each statement, rate yourself on a scale of 1–5:
1: Rarely/Never
2: Occasionally
3: Sometimes
4: Often
5: Almost Always/Always

Part 1: Instructional Leadership (40 points)
1. I articulate a clear and compelling vision for teaching and learning
2. I regularly observe classroom instruction and provide meaningful feedback
3. I use student achievement data to inform school improvement efforts
4. I ensure curriculum alignment with standards and best practices
5. I create structures that promote teacher collaboration and professional learning
6. I model continuous learning by engaging in my own professional development
7. I celebrate and recognize instructional excellence
8. I allocate resources based on instructional priorities

Total points in Part 1:
Percentage Score (Total Points/40):
Reflection: What are my strengths and growth areas as an instructional leader?

Part 2: School Culture and Climate (40 points)
1. I foster a positive, inclusive school culture where all feel valued
2. I actively build trusting relationships with staff, students, and families
3. I communicate high expectations for all students and staff
4. I address issues of equity proactively
5. I promote a culture of innovation and responsible risk-taking
6. I ensure school safety (physical, emotional, and intellectual) is a priority
7. I recognize and celebrate school community successes
8. I model and reinforce the values I want to see throughout the school

Total points in Part 2:
Percentage Score (Total Points/40):
Reflection: How effectively am I shaping a positive school culture and climate?

Part 3: Human Resource Leadership (40 points)
1. I recruit and retain high-quality staff who reflect the diversity of our students
2. I provide meaningful feedback that helps staff improve their practice
3. I identify and develop potential leaders within the staff
4. I address performance concerns directly and supportively
5. I delegate effectively and empower others to lead
6. I differentiate support based on individual needs and experience levels
7. I create conditions that support staff well-being and work-life balance
8. I make difficult personnel decisions when necessary for student welfare

Total points in Part 3:
Percentage Score (Total Points/40):
Reflection: How effectively am I developing my staff and utilizing human resources?

(Continued)

Part 4: Strategic Leadership (40 points)
1. I develop and implement a data-informed strategic plan
2. I anticipate challenges and proactively address them
3. I manage change processes thoughtfully and inclusively
4. I align resources (time, money, people) with strategic priorities
5. I monitor progress toward goals and adjust strategies as needed
6. I balance short-term needs with long-term vision
7. I make decisions based on what's best for student learning
8. I seek diverse perspectives when making important decisions

Total points in Part 4:
Percentage Score (Total Points/40):
Reflection: How effectively am I leading strategic planning and implementation?

Part 5: Community Engagement (40 points)
1. I build productive partnerships with families
2. I engage effectively with diverse community stakeholders
3. I communicate clearly and regularly with all stakeholders
4. I leverage community resources to benefit students
5. I respond constructively to community concerns and feedback
6. I represent the school positively in the broader community
7. I ensure the school is responsive to community needs and contexts
8. I create meaningful opportunities for family involvement

Total points in Part 5:
Percentage Score (Total Points/40):
Reflection: How effectively am I engaging with families and the community?

Part 6: Operational Management (40 points)
1. I develop and manage the school budget effectively
2. I ensure school facilities support the learning environment
3. I implement efficient systems and procedures
4. I comply with district, state, and federal requirements
5. I use technology to enhance organizational effectiveness
6. I delegate operational tasks appropriately
7. I anticipate and plan for potential crises
8. I make data-informed decisions about resource allocation

Total points in Part 6:
Percentage Score (Total Points/40):
Reflection: How effectively am I managing school operations?

Part 7: Personal Leadership (40 points)
1. I demonstrate ethical behavior in all aspects of leadership
2. I maintain composure during stressful situations
3. I balance competing demands effectively
4. I reflect regularly on my leadership practices
5. I seek feedback on my performance from multiple sources
6. I manage my time effectively and prioritize appropriately
7. I maintain appropriate work-life balance and model self-care
8. I demonstrate resilience in the face of challenges

Total points in Part 7:
Percentage Score (Total Points/40):
Reflection: How effectively am I managing myself as a leader?

Table 15.2 School Leader Constituent Feedback

For each statement, rate the school leader on a scale of 1–5.
  1: Rarely/Never
  2: Occasionally
  3: Sometimes
  4: Often
  5: Almost Always/Always
If you have no basis for judgment, please put NA and remove that question from the scoring.

Part 1: Instructional Leadership (40 points)
  1. Articulates a clear and compelling vision for teaching and learning
  2. Regularly observes classroom instruction and provides meaningful feedback
  3. Uses student achievement data to inform school improvement efforts
  4. Ensures curriculum is aligned with standards and best practices
  5. Creates structures that promote teacher collaboration and professional learning
  6. Models continuous learning by engaging in professional development
  7. Celebrates and recognizes instructional excellence
  8. Allocates resources based on instructional priorities
Total points in Part 1:
Percentage Score (Total Points/Total Points Possible without NA responses):
Comments:

Part 2: School Culture and Climate (40 points)
  1. Fosters a positive, inclusive school culture where all feel valued
  2. Actively builds trusting relationships with staff, students, and families
  3. Communicates high expectations for all students and staff
  4. Address issues of equity proactively
  5. Promotes a culture of innovation and responsible risk-taking
  6. Ensures school safety (physical, emotional, and intellectual) is a priority
  7. Recognizes and celebrates school community successes
  8. Models and reinforces the values I want to see throughout the school
Total points in Part 2:
Percentage Score (Total Points/Total Points Possible without NA responses):
Comments:

Part 3: Human Resource Leadership (40 points)
  1. Recruits and retains high-quality staff who reflect the diversity of our students
  2. Provides meaningful feedback that helps staff improve their practice
  3. Identifies and develops potential leaders within the staff
  4. Addresses performance concerns directly and supportively
  5. Delegates effectively and empowers others to lead
  6. Differentiates support based on individual needs and experience levels
  7. Creates conditions that support staff well-being and work-life balance
  8. Makes difficult personnel decisions when necessary for student welfare
Total points in Part 3:
Percentage Score (Total Points/Total Points Possible without NA responses):
Comments:

(*Continued*)

Part 4: Strategic Leadership (40 points)
1. Develops and implements a data-informed strategic plan
2. Anticipates challenges and proactively addresses them
3. Manages change processes thoughtfully and inclusively
4. Aligns resources (time, money, people) with strategic priorities
5. Monitors progress toward goals and adjusts strategies as needed
6. Balances short-term needs with long-term vision
7. Makes decisions based on what's best for student learning
8. Seeks diverse perspectives when making important decisions

Total points in Part 4:
Percentage Score (Total Points/Total Points Possible without NA responses):
Comments:

Part 5: Community Engagement (40 points)
1. Builds productive partnerships with families
2. Engages effectively with diverse community stakeholders
3. Communicate clearly and regularly with all stakeholders
4. Leverages community resources to benefit students
5. Responds constructively to community concerns and feedback
6. Represents the school positively in the broader community
7. Ensures the school is responsive to community needs and contexts
8. Creates meaningful opportunities for family involvement

Total points in Part 5:
Percentage Score (Total Points/Total Points Possible without NA responses):
Comments:

Part 6: Operational Management (40 points)
1. Develops and manages the school budget effectively
2. Ensures school facilities support the learning environment
3. Implements efficient systems and procedures
4. Complies with district, state, and federal requirements
5. Uses technology to enhance organizational effectiveness
6. Delegates operational tasks appropriately
7. Anticipates and plans for potential crises
8. Makes data-informed decisions about resource allocation

Total points in Part 6:
Percentage Score (Total Points/Total Points Possible without NA responses):
Comments:

Part 7: Personal Leadership (40 points)
1. Demonstrates ethical behavior in all aspects of leadership
2. Maintains composure during stressful situations
3. Balances competing demands effectively
4. Reflects regularly on their own leadership practices
5. Seeks feedback on their own performance from multiple sources
6. Manages their time effectively and prioritizes appropriately
7. Maintains appropriate work-life balance and models self-care
8. Demonstrates resilience in the face of challenges

Total points in Part 7:
Percentage Score (Total Points/Total Points Possible without NA responses):
Comments:

The scores should not be considered a "grade" per se; this is merely to provide you with some idea as to where your strengths and areas of growth may lie so you can develop an effective improvement plan.

After completing the scoring, look at your percentage score in each part, for both the self-assessment and the constituent feedback. How do your scores compare with those given to you by others? Do others perceive you as you perceive yourself? Identify the disconnects between your scores and those of constituents. How might you bridge those gaps?

With your scoring completed, identify three strengths and three areas for growth indicated in the assessment. Most importantly, consider how your responses impact

- Student learning and achievement
- Staff effectiveness and morale
- School culture and climate
- Community engagement and perception

Based on your identified strengths and areas of growth, answer the following questions:

- What are two to three specific leadership goals I will pursue in the next six to twelve months?
- What professional learning experiences will help me achieve these goals?
- What resources or support will I need to grow in these areas?
- How will I measure progress toward these goals?

After a rigorous self-assessment, complemented by input from others and resulting in a plan developed in response to the questions above, you will be on the path toward continual improvement. This is a critical step for leaders in any field. When we become complacent—content with our current level of performance or resting on the laurels of past accomplishments—we are, in fact, failing ourselves and our schools.

It is when we convince ourselves that we have this work all figured out that we are most likely to stumble, which is something we can ill afford given all that is at stake in schools. Remaining open to the call for career-long learning is the necessary approach for continual improvement—in ourselves and in our schools.

Staff, students, and communities rely on school leaders to lead with intent. That begins with purposeful assessment of your own performance, deliberate effort to engage and empower those around you, and purposeful planning to cohesively and consistently move the school forward toward its intended mission. With the right approach and intentional effort in each moment, you can confidently and collaboratively ensure that the students you serve will be provided the best opportunities to meet their highest goals.

Bibliography

"2024 Edelman Trust Barometer," The Edleman Group (November 24, 2024). Retrieved from https://www.edelman.com/sites/g/files/aatuss191/files/2024-02/2024%20Edelman%20Trust%20Barometer%20Global%20Report_FINAL.pdf.

Aveling, G., *The Ritz-Carlton Experience: It's All in the Implementation* (July 2009). Retrieved from http://www.brandingasia.com/columns/017.htm.

Collins, J., *Good to Great: Why Some Companies Make the Leap... and Others Don't* (London: Harper Business, 2001).

Dolloff, A., *The Trust Imperative: Practical Approaches to Effective School Leadership* (Baltimore, MD: Rowman & Littlefield, 2022).

Elmore, R., "Building a New Structure for School Leadership," Lecture presented at the Harvard Graduate School of Education's Principals Center (Cambridge, MA, July 8, 2003).

Feldman, J., *Grading for Equity: What It Is, Why It Matters, and How It Can Transform Schools and Classrooms* (Thousand Oaks, CA: Corwin Press, 2018).

Gardner, D. P., *A Nation at Risk: The Imperative for Educational Reform. An Open Letter to the American People. A Report to the Nation and the Secretary of Education.* National Commission on Excellence in Education (ED) (Washington, DC, April 1983). Retrieved from https://eric.ed.gov/?id=ED226006.

Hattie, J., *Visible Learning for Teachers: Maximizing Impact on Learning* (Oxfordshire, England: Routledge, 2012).

Jenkins, D., "IST of an ISM: 'Systemically Dominant and Systemically Non-Dominant," *Share the Flame* (2025). Retrieved from https://www.shareflame.com/.

Klien, G., "Performing a Project Pre-mortem," *Harvard Business Review* (2007). Retrieved from https://hbr.org/2007/09/performing-a-project-premortem.

Noguera, P., "Standards for What? Accountability for Whom?" Lecture presented at the Harvard Graduate School of Education's Principals Center (Cambridge, MA, July 9, 2003).

"Poll of the Public's Attitudes toward the Public Schools 2022," Phi Delta Kappa, last modified (June 25, 2022). Retrieved from https://pdkpoll.org/2022-pdk-poll-results/.

"Public Trust in Government: 1958–2024," Pew Research Center, last modified (June 24, 2024). Retrieved from https://www.pewresearch.org/politics/2024/06/24/public-trust-in-government-1958-2024/.

Ratanjee, V., "How to Build Trust in the Workplace," *Gallup.com* (June 14, 2022). Retrieved from https://www.gallup.com/workplace/393401/trust-decline-rebuild.aspx.

Zak, P. J., *Trust Factor: The Science of Creating High-Performance Companies* (New York: AMACOM, 2017).

About the Author

Dr. Andrew Dolloff is a thirty-eight-year veteran of public schools, having begun his career as a high school chemistry teacher and serving in a range of leadership positions from faculty chairperson and Athletic Director to High School Principal. For the past sixteen years, Andrew has served as Superintendent of Schools in two Prek-12 public school districts.

Andrew has led three National Blue Ribbon Schools of Excellence and at various points in his career has been recognized as Maine Principal of the Year and Maine Superintendent of the Year, along with numerous other regional awards.

Andrew has served on the International Advisory Board for the Harvard Graduate School of Education's Principals' Center, the New England School Development Council (NESDEC), and the University of Southern Maine's Educational Leadership Advisory Board, where he is an adjunct professor of educational leadership.

Andrew's first book, *The Trust Imperative*, was released in 2022 and is being used in leadership preparatory programs and professional development settings as a resource for aspiring and veteran school leaders.

Andrew is an engaging keynote speaker, workshop presenter, and leadership consultant who travels throughout the United States to work with school leaders at all levels to sharpen their focus on trust-filled schools.

You can learn more about Andrew's work by visiting www.trustimperative.org or scanning the QR code provided here.

Figure A.1. Andrew Dolloff, PhD.